Russia

Czech Republic

Greece

Persia
(now Iran)

Japan

China

India

Africa

Cambodia

Australia

New Zealand

Usborne

Stories from Around the World

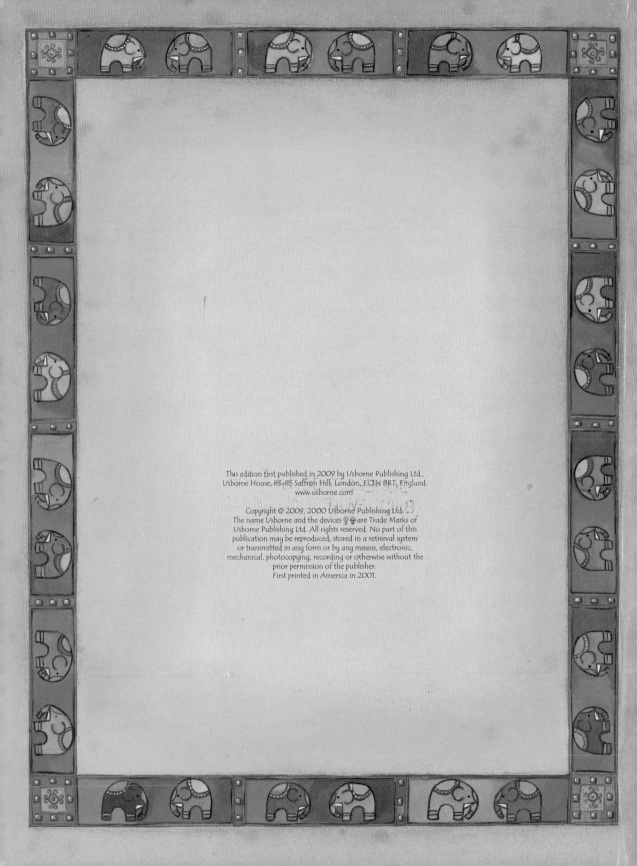

This edition first published in 2009 by Usborne Publishing Ltd.,
Usborne House, 83-85 Saffron Hill, London, EC1N 8RT, England.
www.usborne.com

Usborne
Stories from Around the World

Retold by Heather Amery
Illustrated by Linda Edwards

Designed by Joe Pedley
Edited by Michelle Bates
& Jenny Tyler

Contents

Contents

Strong Magic

A story from Australia

Long, long ago there was a boy who had no mother or father. He lived with his tribe, and was often very naughty. "That boy," they would mutter angrily. "He's a lazy, good-for-nothing who never does as he's told. He won't work and he's up to all sorts of tricks."

When the dry season came there was no water in the streams, rivers and ponds, and the people had to walk a long way to the boreholes for drinking water. The boy didn't like walking. He stayed in the camp and, when the water-carriers came back, he would beg them for a drink. They always gave him one, but soon the time came when they were really angry with

6

the lazy boy. "Go and get your own water," they shouted and they hid their water bowls.

One morning, when the men went off hunting and the women and children went to dig for roots to eat, the boy was left alone in the camp. He played around for a while, but began to feel really thirsty. He looked in the usual places for the water bowls, but they weren't there. Eventually, he found them hidden under a bush, and had a good, long drink.

Then he thought of a naughty trick. "I'll hide the water bowls where those mean people won't be able to find them. Then I can have a drink whenever I like," he said to himself.

One by one, he carried the full bowls of water to a small gum tree. Quickly, he climbed up the tree and hid the bowls among the leaves. He was just putting the last one on a branch when,

by some strong, strange magic, the tree started to grow up and up. The boy clung to a branch as the tree grew taller and taller until it was huge. When it stopped growing, the boy was right at the very top with all of the water bowls.

In the evening, when everyone came back to the camp, they all wanted a drink, but when they looked under the bush they found only a few empty water bowls.

"It's that boy. He's been up to his tricks again. Where is he?" they grumbled. They looked around and saw the huge gum tree that, only that morning, had been a little

8

tree. At the top, they saw the boy with their full water bowls.

"Bring down our water at once," they shouted. "If you want your water, you'll have to come and get it," the boy shouted back.

Two young men began to climb the tree. When they had almost reached the boy, he wailed and moaned with fright. One of the men stretched up to grab him but, as the boy tried to get away, he slipped and fell down the tree…

…bump, bump, bump, right down to the ground.

There he lay for a moment, bruised and aching. Then he scrambled up the gum tree again to escape from the angry tribe. Some people began to climb up after him but, by some strong, strange magic, they saw him start to change.

9

Thick fur covered his body. His ears became like black buttons and his nose black and shiny. He looked just like a bear. He had turned into the very first koala!

From that time on, all koalas have lived in gum trees. If they are thirsty, they eat a few leaves instead of going down to look for water, and if anyone tries to climb their trees, they moan and wail, just like that naughty boy.

Leyla and the Lamp

A story from Persia

Long ago, in the old city of Tabriz, a rich merchant lived with his only daughter. Her name was Leyla, and she was sweet-tempered and very pretty.

One day, the merchant said to Leyla. " It's time you had a husband. I want you to marry my friend, Mamood. His wife has died and he wants a new wife. He's very rich and you would have a fine house, jewels and as many beautiful clothes as you would like." Leyla was horrified. "Oh please, please don't make me marry him.

He's old, fat and ugly, and everyone knows he was very cruel to his wife. I would rather die than have him for a husband."

The merchant frowned. "Leyla," he said angrily, "Tomorrow I have to go away for four days. When I return, I want you to marry Mamood. Be a good girl and do as your father wishes."

Leyla couldn't sleep that night. She tossed and turned in her bed, crying, but also thinking hard. When it was just growing light, she had thought of a plan. After breakfast, she said to her father, "I would like a new lamp for my room. While you are away, may I have one made?"

The merchant was pleased that Leyla seemed in a good mood. "Of course, my dear," he said, "I'll order the lamp-maker to come to the house. You can have anything that you like." Then he kissed Leyla and set out on his journey.

When the lamp-maker came, Leyla told him exactly what she wanted, and three days later, the lamp was delivered. It was very tall, had forty smaller lamps around the top and a secret door in the base.

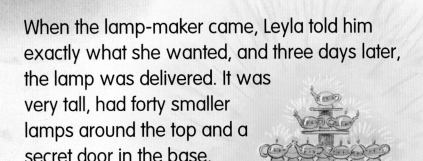

That night, when all the servants were asleep, Leyla crept out of the house. She took off her shoes, left one by the well and dropped the other into the water. Then she tiptoed back to her room. She opened the secret door in the lamp, put in a good supply of food and water, stepped in and closed the door behind her.

Later that week, the merchant came home and called to

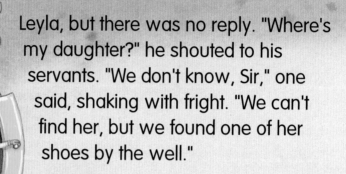

Leyla, but there was no reply. "Where's my daughter?" he shouted to his servants. "We don't know, Sir," one said, shaking with fright. "We can't find her, but we found one of her shoes by the well."

"Oh Leyla, Leyla, my darling daughter," cried the merchant. "What have I done? You said you'd rather die than marry Mamood and now you've drowned yourself." The merchant went to Leyla's room and cried, and cried. Then he noticed the lamp. "Take that thing to the bazaar and sell it. I can't bear to look at it. It reminds me of Leyla," he shouted to his servants. The servants carried the lamp away, grumbling about the weight.

At the bazaar, a young and handsome prince strolled among the stalls with his servants.

He stopped when he saw the lamp and asked the price. After much bargaining, he bought it and had it carried to his palace.

The prince liked to eat breakfast alone in his room each morning so every evening his servants would lay the table with food and drink so that it was ready for him. The first morning that the prince had his new lamp, he was surprised to see that all of his breakfast had been eaten, and only a few crumbs were left. The same thing happened the next morning; the breakfast was eaten. That night, the prince decided he would stay awake and try to catch the thief. He went to bed as usual, put out the light and pretended to be asleep.

Just as it was starting to get light, he saw the secret door in the lamp open, and a girl creep out. "Now I've caught you," shouted the prince, leaping out of bed. Leyla screamed and tried to jump back into the lamp, but the prince slammed the door shut. The prince gazed at the trembling girl. "Don't be frightened, I won't hurt you," he said gently. "Come and sit down, and tell me why you were hiding."

Through her tears, Leyla told the prince all about her father, how he wanted her to marry his friend, Mamood, and how she had planned her escape. "You're a brave and clever girl," said the prince, smiling. "Dry your tears and let's have some breakfast together. Then we must decide what to do."

All that day, Leyla and the prince talked and walked together in the garden, thinking up all sorts of plans, and laughing at the silly ones. At last, the prince kissed Leyla's hand and said, "I would like to marry you. Let's go and see your father tomorrow." Leyla was so happy that she could only nod.

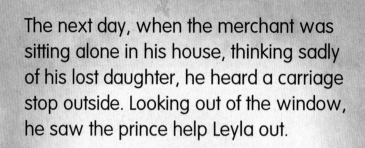

The next day, when the merchant was sitting alone in his house, thinking sadly of his lost daughter, he heard a carriage stop outside. Looking out of the window, he saw the prince help Leyla out.

With a great cry of joy he rushed to the door, opened it and flung his arms around Leyla. "My daughter, oh, my darling daughter, you're alive. How wonderful. Come in, come in."

In the house, Leyla introduced her father to the prince and told him all about the lamp and the secret door. Her father was so pleased to see her again that he forgave her for the trick that she had played on him, and happily agreed she should marry the prince. He arranged a splendid wedding for them, and gave them the lamp as a present.

How the Turtle got its Shell

A story from Greece

The great god Zeus was the ruler of all the Greek gods. He was so powerful and could be so bad-tempered, always flinging thunderbolts around, that the other gods were a little scared of him.

When Zeus was getting married, he invited all of the animals to a huge wedding feast. The great day came and the animals set off, barking and braying, snorting and squealing, growling and grunting, whinnying and whistling with excitement. They had a wonderful time. For a whole day they ate as much as they could of all the foods they liked best.

Zeus looked at them, smiling with pleasure. Then he frowned. "Where's the turtle?" he asked Hera, his new wife. "Why isn't she here?"

Hera was a goddess and could see at once that the turtle was not with all the other animals. "I'll go and ask her tomorrow," said Zeus.

The next day, Zeus found the turtle, resting quietly on the muddy bank of a river. "Turtle, why, of all the animals, didn't you come to my wedding feast?" he asked in a gentle voice.

The turtle tried to hide under a big leaf growing on the river bank, and said nothing. "Why didn't you come to my wedding feast? Answer me," Zeus demanded. The turtle raised her head and whispered in a tiny, scared voice, "There's no place like home."

Zeus was furious. He shouted in a voice so loud it frightened the birds which flew screaming and shrieking away through the forest, "In that case, you will always carry your home with you wherever you go." Then he disappeared with a crash of thunder and a flash of blinding light.

The turtle suddenly felt a great weight on her back. It was a hard, heavy shell which covered her all over. She scuttled off, with only her scaly head, the tip of her tail, and her four bent legs showing from under it. From then on, all the turtles in the world have always carried their homes on their backs.

Puss in Boots

A story from France

An old miller, who lived in Provence, had three sons. When he died, the miller left the mill to his eldest son, his donkey to his second son, and to his youngest son, he left his cat.

The two eldest sons were pleased because, together, they could earn a good living with the mill and the donkey. The youngest son grumbled as he walked away from the mill. "My brothers will eat well, but I'll soon die of hunger. All I have is a useless cat."

"Master," purred the cat, "I'm not useless. Just give me a sack and a pair of boots, and you'll soon see how useful I can be."

The son stared at the cat, but the cat just purred at him. "Oh very well, but it's a waste of the only money I have," he muttered angrily as he walked to the village to find a sack and have a pair of boots made.

The cat put on the boots, took the sack and marched away to a grassy hill full of rabbit burrows. He put fresh leaves in the sack, left it open, and hid behind a bush. Soon the rabbits came out to feed, and one hopped into the sack to eat the leaves. The cat leaped out and grabbed the sack. Slinging it over his shoulder, he marched off to the King's palace.

The cat bowed low before the King and said, "Your Majesty, I bring you a gift from my master, the Marquis de Carabas." The King was pleased, and sent the rabbit to the kitchens to be cooked for his dinner.

Each day, for a whole week, the cat took something that he'd caught to the King. One day it was a pheasant, another day it was two partridges, and another day it was a huge fish. Each time he bowed and said, "A gift from the Marquis de Carabas, your Majesty." The King was delighted.

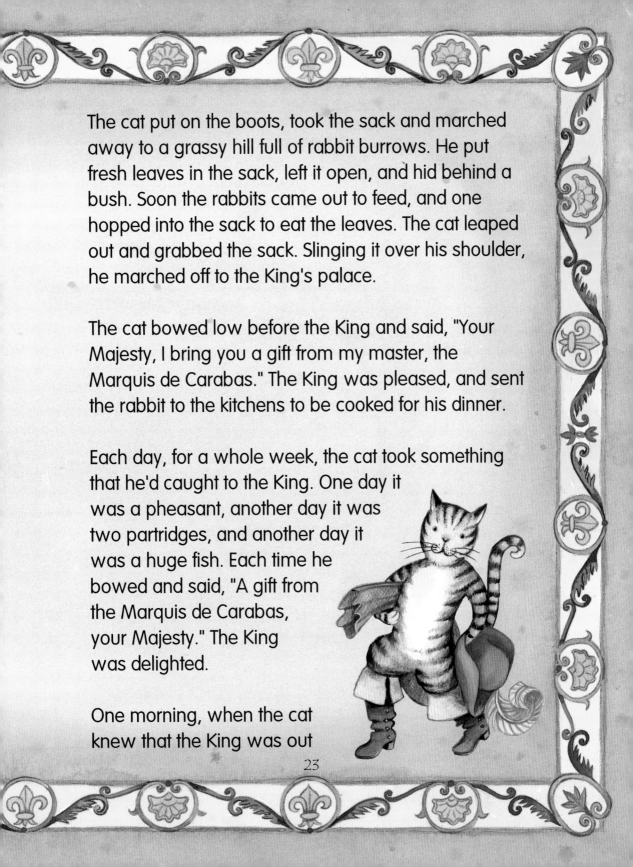

One morning, when the cat knew that the King was out

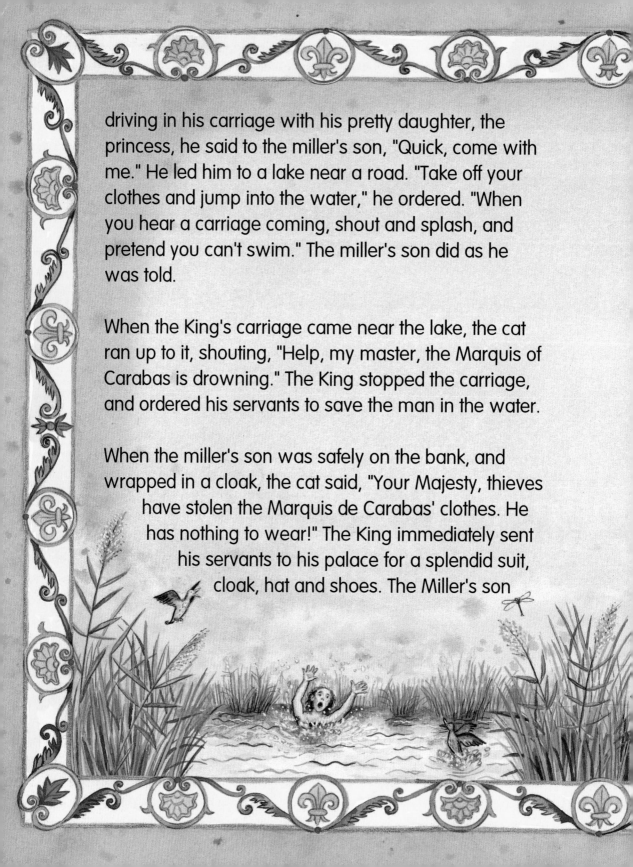

driving in his carriage with his pretty daughter, the princess, he said to the miller's son, "Quick, come with me." He led him to a lake near a road. "Take off your clothes and jump into the water," he ordered. "When you hear a carriage coming, shout and splash, and pretend you can't swim." The miller's son did as he was told.

When the King's carriage came near the lake, the cat ran up to it, shouting, "Help, my master, the Marquis of Carabas is drowning." The King stopped the carriage, and ordered his servants to save the man in the water.

When the miller's son was safely on the bank, and wrapped in a cloak, the cat said, "Your Majesty, thieves have stolen the Marquis de Carabas' clothes. He has nothing to wear!" The King immediately sent his servants to his palace for a splendid suit, cloak, hat and shoes. The Miller's son

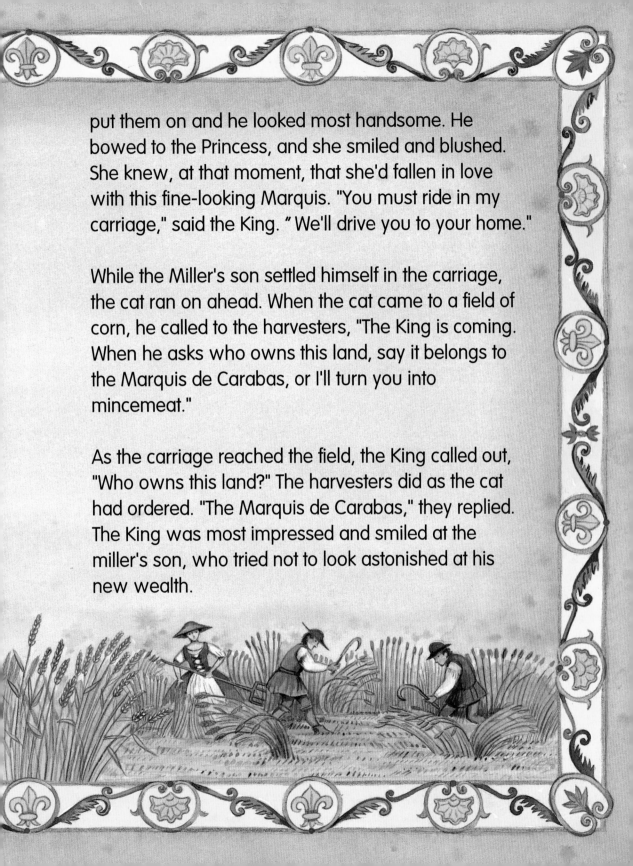

put them on and he looked most handsome. He bowed to the Princess, and she smiled and blushed. She knew, at that moment, that she'd fallen in love with this fine-looking Marquis. "You must ride in my carriage," said the King. "We'll drive you to your home."

While the Miller's son settled himself in the carriage, the cat ran on ahead. When the cat came to a field of corn, he called to the harvesters, "The King is coming. When he asks who owns this land, say it belongs to the Marquis de Carabas, or I'll turn you into mincemeat."

As the carriage reached the field, the King called out, "Who owns this land?" The harvesters did as the cat had ordered. "The Marquis de Carabas," they replied. The King was most impressed and smiled at the miller's son, who tried not to look astonished at his new wealth.

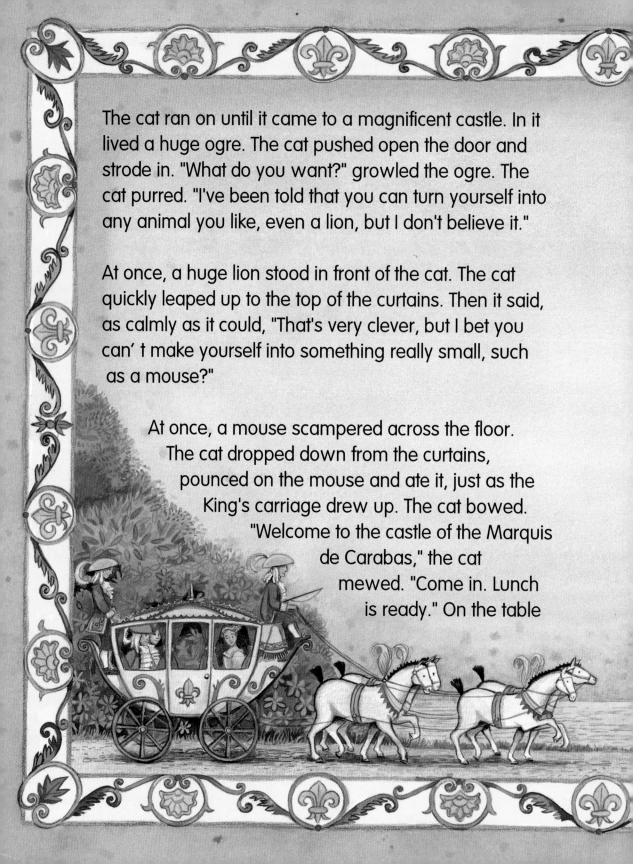

The cat ran on until it came to a magnificent castle. In it lived a huge ogre. The cat pushed open the door and strode in. "What do you want?" growled the ogre. The cat purred. "I've been told that you can turn yourself into any animal you like, even a lion, but I don't believe it."

At once, a huge lion stood in front of the cat. The cat quickly leaped up to the top of the curtains. Then it said, as calmly as it could, "That's very clever, but I bet you can' t make yourself into something really small, such as a mouse?"

At once, a mouse scampered across the floor. The cat dropped down from the curtains, pounced on the mouse and ate it, just as the King's carriage drew up. The cat bowed. "Welcome to the castle of the Marquis de Carabas," the cat mewed. "Come in. Lunch is ready." On the table was a wonderful feast that the ogre had prepared for himself. Trying to behave like a Marquis, the miller's son helped the Princess down from the carriage. The King gazed at the castle, and the land and farms all around it. "The Marquis de Carabas must be very rich, and would make an excellent husband for my daughter," he said to himself.

The "Marquis" led the King and the Princess into the castle, thinking, "The Princess would be a lovely wife for me."

Soon the miller's son, now quite used to being the Marquis de Carabas, and the Princess were married, and lived very happily in the castle. The cat lived with them, and never had to chase a mouse again, unless, of course, it couldn't think of anything better to do!

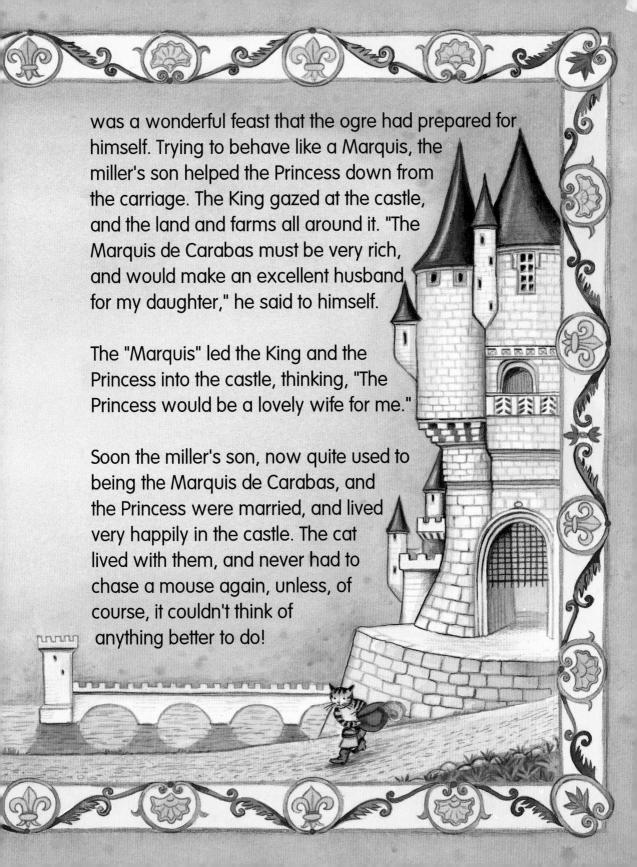

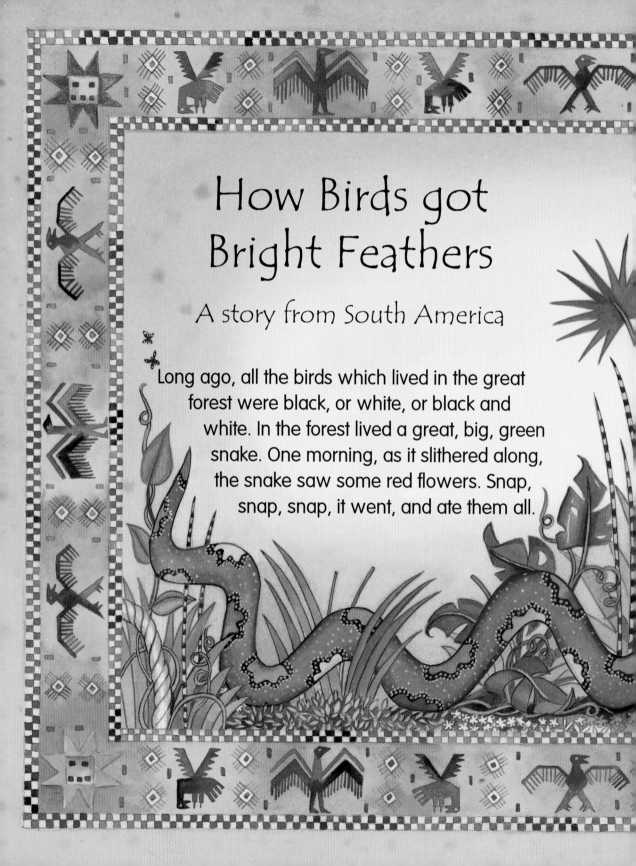

How Birds got Bright Feathers

A story from South America

Long ago, all the birds which lived in the great
forest were black, or white, or black and
white. In the forest lived a great, big, green
snake. One morning, as it slithered along,
the snake saw some red flowers. Snap,
snap, snap, it went, and ate them all.

As it glided on, the snake caught sight of its tail. It turned its head to have a better look. Along its body were patches of red. "Strange," thought the snake, "but it looks good."

Later, the snake came to some blue flowers. Crunch, crunch, crunch, it ate them all. Then it turned its head to look at its body. Yes, bright blue patches were beginning to appear. The snake was delighted. It wound its way right through the forest, snapping up every flower it found.

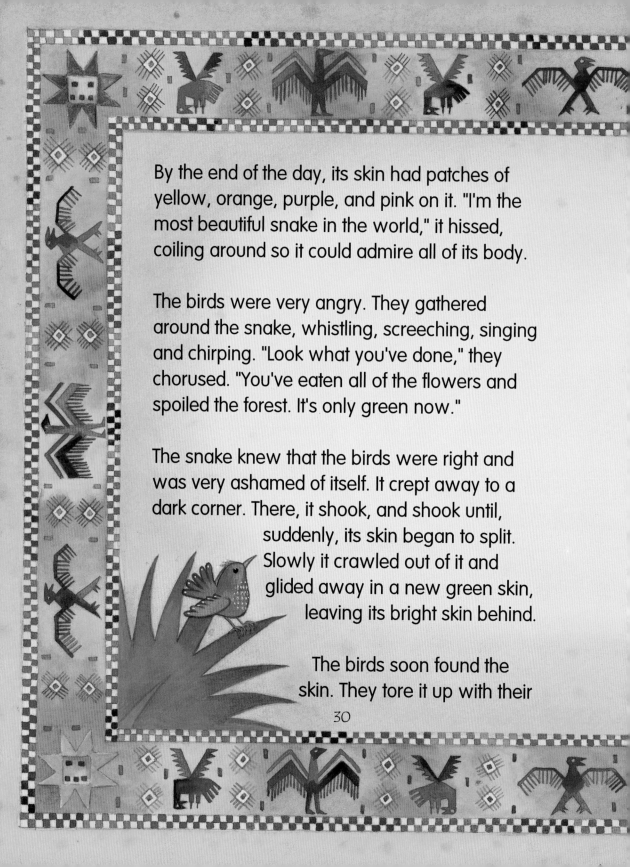

By the end of the day, its skin had patches of yellow, orange, purple, and pink on it. "I'm the most beautiful snake in the world," it hissed, coiling around so it could admire all of its body.

The birds were very angry. They gathered around the snake, whistling, screeching, singing and chirping. "Look what you've done," they chorused. "You've eaten all of the flowers and spoiled the forest. It's only green now."

The snake knew that the birds were right and was very ashamed of itself. It crept away to a dark corner. There, it shook, and shook until, suddenly, its skin began to split. Slowly it crawled out of it and glided away in a new green skin, leaving its bright skin behind.

The birds soon found the skin. They tore it up with their

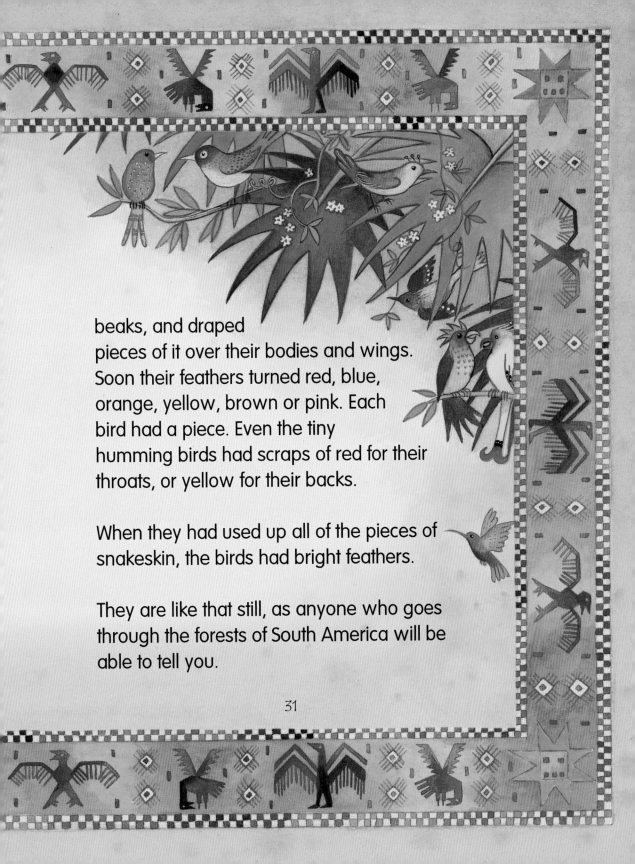

beaks, and draped
pieces of it over their bodies and wings.
Soon their feathers turned red, blue,
orange, yellow, brown or pink. Each
bird had a piece. Even the tiny
humming birds had scraps of red for their
throats, or yellow for their backs.

When they had used up all of the pieces of
snakeskin, the birds had bright feathers.

They are like that still, as anyone who goes
through the forests of South America will be
able to tell you.

The Magic Fish Hook

A story from New Zealand

Long ago and far away on an island in Polynesia, Taranga married one of the many gods who lived there. She was happy and, in time, she had four strong healthy sons. Then she had another son who she called Maui. But, instead of being happy, she felt very sad. For Maui was thin and weak and, at that time, any sickly baby had to be put outside to die.

Taranga loved her little son, and was desperate to find a way to save him. One dark night she picked Maui up and crept out of the sleeping longhouse, down to the seashore. There she found a piece of bone. She scratched "Maui" on it, and hung it around the baby's neck. Then she made a cradle of floating seaweed, put Maui in it, kissed him, and pushed it out onto the dark sea. "May the gods look after you," she whispered.

When Taranga crept back into the longhouse, her husband had gone. Taranga had broken the law, and he had left her; she would never see him again. The cradle, with Maui fast asleep in it, floated away on the sea, and was washed up far away on a beach. In the morning, Tama, a wise old fisherman, found the baby. He read the name on the piece of bone.

"Maui, I feel in my heart that you are a very special boy," he whispered. Gently, he picked up the sleeping baby and carried him back to his house. There, he fed him, and looked after him.

In time, Maui grew from a thin, weak baby into a strong, healthy boy. Tama taught him everything he could. He taught him how to fish, how to understand the language of birds and animals, and even to know what other people were thinking.

When Maui was twelve years old, Tama said, "My dear boy, it's time you went to live with your own family." Sadly, Maui said goodbye to the kind old man, and set off on his journey.

At last, he came to his longhouse. His mother saw the piece of bone around his neck, and knew at once that this was her son. She hugged him and kissed him, laughing with joy. "The gods have sent you back to me," she cried, taking Maui into the longhouse.

But Maui's four brothers weren't so pleased to see him. After a few days, they grew jealous of Maui. "Our mother loves that brat more than us," they muttered. "Let us find a way to make her think he's a spoiled, lazy boy." Secretly whispering together, they made a plan to go fishing very early next morning, and when they came back, they would tell their mother that Maui was too lazy to go with them. Maui knew what they were thinking, and made his own plan.

He got up before dawn the next morning, and crept down to the seashore. There, he hid in his brothers' fishing canoe, covering himself with nets. His brothers came at dawn, and paddled the canoe out to sea.

Maui heard one of them say, "Maui is still asleep. Now our mother will know how lazy he is." Maui sat up. "I'm not lazy," he laughed. The brothers were angry that he was in their canoe, but there was nothing that they could do about it. They began to fish, and fished for hours, but they caught nothing. "Paddle further out to sea," said Maui, "I'll catch the fish there."

The brothers scowled and muttered, but they paddled out from the shore until they were a long way out at sea. "Since you're so clever, let's see you catch fish," one brother said, angrily.

Maui smiled to himself, tied a magic fish hook to a long line, and gently dropped it over the side of the canoe. For a while, nothing happened, and the brothers jeered at Maui. "We've paddled all the way out here but you' re no better at catching fish than we are," one growled. Then, suddenly, there was a huge tug on the line. "Help me pull it in," shouted Maui.

Together the five brothers heaved on the line. It was so heavy, they pulled and pulled for hours. At last, they could see something rising slowly in the water. "It must be a giant fish," shouted one brother. Another peered over the side of the canoe. "No," he shouted. "It's an island. Maui has fished up an island."

It was a beautiful, green island, shaped almost like a fish. It rose up in the sea until it floated on the top. The four brothers jumped onto it, shouting at each other, "This part is mine. I'm the eldest, I should have the biggest piece. No, this is mine. I got here first. I'm going to have this part."

Then they started fighting, battering the island, throwing up mountains and gouging out valleys. Suddenly, there was a crack like thunder, and the island split in two.

The four brothers were so scared at what they had done, they jumped into their canoe, and paddled away back to their home. Maui watched them go and smiled. He had made a new land where his people could live. It's called New Zealand. If you look at a map and imagine how the two islands would look joined together, you can see that it does look a little like a fish.

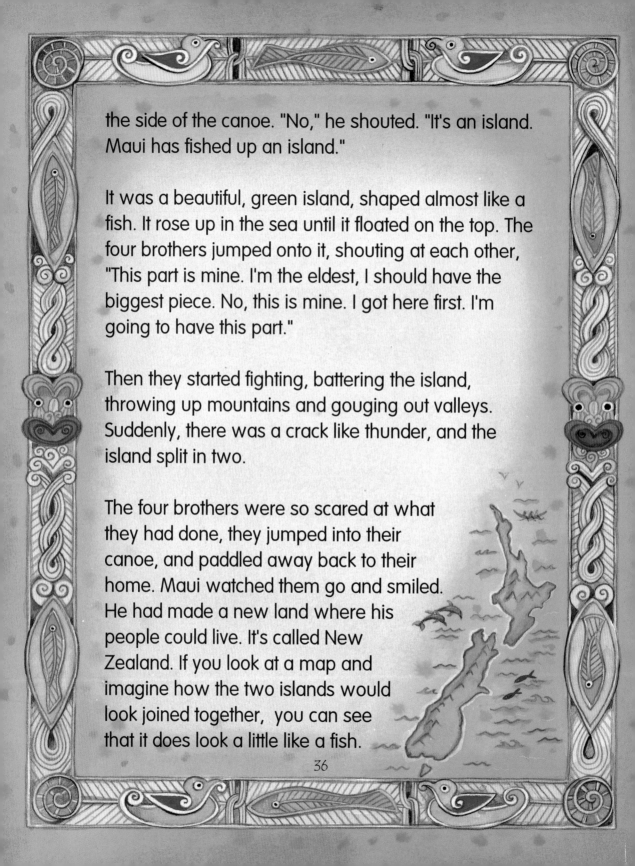

The Musicians of Bremen

A story from Germany

Very early one morning, a donkey left his home on a farm and trotted along the road to the German city of Bremen. The donkey had worked very hard for his master for many years but now he was old and tired. He knew his master had no use for him any more so the donkey had decided to earn his living by becoming a musician in the town band of Bremen.

After an hour or so, the donkey saw an old hunting dog lying by the side of the road, yawning and sighing. The donkey stopped. "What's the matter, my friend? Why are you yawning and sighing like that?"

"Oh dear," sighed the dog, "I'm too old to hunt any more. My master beats me every day so I've run away. Now, I'm just going to have to lie here and starve to death."

"I'm going to Bremen to play in the town band," the donkey brayed. "Come with me. I'll play the lute and you can bang on the drum." The old dog thought for a moment, then he got to his feet, and the donkey and the dog trotted away down the road together.

After another hour or so, they met a cat sitting beside the road, looking very, very miserable. The donkey and the dog stopped in front of her. "Why are you so long-faced and sad?" asked the donkey. "I'm growing too old to catch mice," mewed the cat. "I'd rather sit by the fire and sleep. My mistress wants to drown me, so I've run away, and now I don't know what to do."

"Come with us to Bremen," said the donkey. "We're going there to join the town band. I know that you sing at night so you could be a musician too."

The cat agreed and together the donkey, the dog and the cat

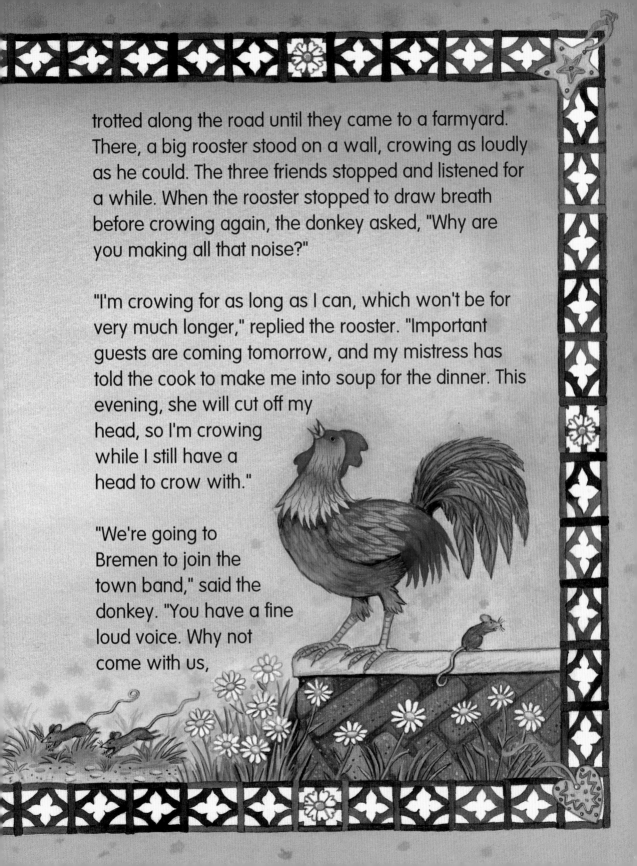

trotted along the road until they came to a farmyard. There, a big rooster stood on a wall, crowing as loudly as he could. The three friends stopped and listened for a while. When the rooster stopped to draw breath before crowing again, the donkey asked, "Why are you making all that noise?"

"I'm crowing for as long as I can, which won't be for very much longer," replied the rooster. "Important guests are coming tomorrow, and my mistress has told the cook to make me into soup for the dinner. This evening, she will cut off my head, so I'm crowing while I still have a head to crow with."

"We're going to Bremen to join the town band," said the donkey. "You have a fine loud voice. Why not come with us,

and we can all make music."
The rooster thought for a moment,
scratching his head with one claw. "It's better than
being made into soup," he crowed, and the donkey,
the dog, the cat and the rooster trotted away down the
road to Bremen.

It was a long way to the city and, by the evening, the
four friends came to a dark forest. "We'll have to stay
here for the night," brayed the donkey. He and the dog
lay down on some dry leaves under a tree. The cat
climbed the tree and lay on a branch. The rooster flew
up into the tree and perched on the highest branch.

The rooster was just closing his eyes when he saw a
faint glimmer of light through the trees. "I think I can
see a house," he crowed to his three friends. "Well,

let's go and find it. I don't think much of where we're sleeping," brayed the donkey, standing up. "And I could do with a good dinner," said the dog.

The donkey, the dog, the cat and the rooster crept though the dark forest to the light, which grew brighter and brighter as they got nearer and nearer. The donkey was the tallest of the four animals so he peeped through the window.

"What can you see?" growled the dog, very quietly. "I can see a table laid with food and drinks. Four robbers are sitting around it, having a very good time," whispered the donkey.

"That would suit us very well, but how are we going to get the robbers out so that we can get in?" asked the dog. "We'll have to think of a plan. Has anybody got any ideas?" asked the donkey.

The four friends put their heads together and whispered for a short while. At last, the donkey said, "That's a very good plan. Now, you all know what you have to do, and don't make a sound until I give the signal."

Very quietly, the donkey trotted up to the window and put his front hooves on the window sill. The dog jumped up on his back, the cat climbed up on the dog's back and the rooster flew up and perched on the cat's head. When they were ready, the donkey brayed, the dog barked, the cat meowed and the rooster crowed, all as loudly as they could.

In the cottage, the robbers jumped up from the table, terrified by the deafening noise. They rushed out of the door, pushing each other to get out first, and ran far away into the forest.

The four animals trotted into the cottage and ate all

that was left on the table. Then, tired out, they turned out the light and found somewhere comfortable to sleep. The donkey lay on some straw, the dog settled down behind the door, the cat curled up in front of the glowing ashes in the hearth, and the rooster perched on a beam near the ceiling. Within a few minutes, they were all fast asleep.

Out in the forest, the robbers saw the light go out in the cottage. All was quiet. "Maybe we shouldn't have been scared and run away," said the leader. "You go and find out what's happening in there," he ordered one of the men.

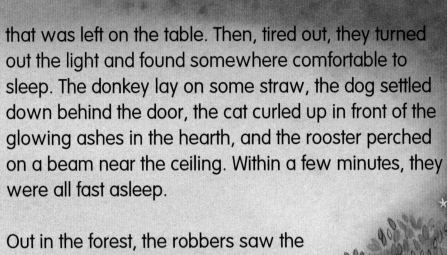

The robber crept through the trees to the cottage, stopped and listened. There wasn't a sound. He pushed open the door and tiptoed into the dark room. He saw the

cat's eyes glowing and thought they were glowing coals. He bent down to blow them into a flame, jumping back as the cat spat at him and scratched his face with her claws. The robber was so scared. He stumbled back towards the door, tripped over the donkey who kicked him on his leg, woke up the dog who bit him on his other leg, and, as he fled the cottage, he heard the startling sound of "cock-a-doodle-do".

The man ran as fast as he could through the forest back to the other robbers. "There's a horrible witch in the cottage," he gasped. "She spat at me and scratched my face with her long nails. A man hit me in the leg with a club and another man behind the door stabbed my other leg with a knife. When I ran out of the cottage, a man shouted, "Crook, what do you do?"

The robbers didn't dare go back to their cottage, even in daylight. In fact they never, ever went back there again. The donkey, the dog, the cat and the rooster never became musicians in the town band in Bremen either. They stayed in the cottage and for all anyone knows, the four animal friends may be there still.

The Singing Toad

A story from Mexico

Every morning, an old farmer and his three sons would walk out in the hot sunshine to see how the corn was growing in their fields. "Soon be ready for harvesting," the farmer would growl.

One morning, when they looked at the corn, they saw that someone, or something, had torn up the plants in one corner of a field, and eaten all of the ripe cobs. "Who's been here in the night?" the farmer shouted, angrily. The three sons searched around but they couldn't find any footprints or any sign of the thief. "Tonight you must watch the field and catch the robber," the old farmer said to his eldest son.

That evening, the eldest son picked up his gun and a corn cake and set off for the field. On the way, he came across a well. Sitting by it was a toad, singing. "Be quiet. You have a horrible voice and that's a horrible song. Be quiet now, or you'll frighten away the thief I've

45

come to catch," the eldest son ordered the toad. "Please give me a piece of your corn cake," croaked the toad. "No, I want it all," shouted the eldest son.

The toad opened its mouth and sang an even louder and longer song. "If you won't be quiet, I'll make you," shouted the eldest son. He picked up the toad and dropped it into the well. Then he walked away and sat down at the edge of the corn field.

All night, he sat by the field but heard and saw nothing. In the early morning, he was amazed to see that more corn plants had been torn up and the cobs eaten. He had to go back to his father and tell him the bad news. "You must go this evening and watch the field," the father said to his second son.

Just as the sun was setting, the second son took his gun and a corn cake and walked to the field. When he reached the well, there was the toad, singing a long, loud song.

"What a terrible noise. Please be quiet,"

46

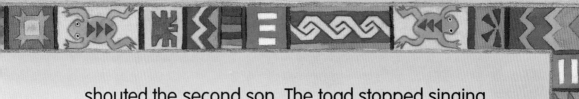

shouted the second son. The toad stopped singing. "Give me a piece of your corn cake, please," it croaked. "No, it's mine and I want it all," said the second son. The toad started to sing again, even louder this time. "That's enough," shouted the second son and, picking up the toad by one leg, he flung it down the well. Then he walked away and sat down by the corn field.

All night, the second son sat by the field of corn, but he heard and saw nothing. In the morning, more corn had been torn up and eaten and he had to tell his father that he hadn't caught the thief.

The next evening, the farmer sent his youngest son to guard the corn. The son walked slowly to the field, afraid that if his two brothers couldn't catch the thief, he, too, would fail. He stopped when he heard the toad singing by the well. "What a fine voice you have, and that's a wonderful song," he said. "Glad you like it," croaked

47

the toad, and sang an even louder and longer song. "Will you give me a piece of your corn cake?" it croaked, when it had finished. "Certainly, help yourself," said the youngest son, and he put the whole cake down in front of the toad.

When the toad had gobbled up the last crumbs, it said, "Since you've been so kind, I'll tell you a secret. At the bottom of this well, there's a magic emerald. It can grant wishes. You may have three wishes."

"Thank you," said the son. He thought for a while. "Can I have anything, anything I like?" he asked. "Anything or anyone," croaked the toad. "Then I would like a wife," said the son. "You'd better decide what sort of wife you' d like before you wish, and you'd better have a house for her to live in," croaked the toad. "Now, lean over the well, say what you wish and don't mumble."

The son looked down the well at the cool water. "I wish for a wife who is kind, beautiful and a good cook, a fine house near the well, and that I catch

48

the corn thief," he said very loudly and very clearly. "Now we must go to the field," croaked the toad. The son picked up the toad, put it on his shoulder, and with the toad singing loudly, walked to the corn field.

The sun was just setting over the distant mountains when a huge white bird appeared in the sky. It flew down to the field and started tearing at the corn cobs. The toad hopped over to it and started to sing a soft, sweet lullaby. The bird stopped eating, closed its eyes and was soon fast asleep. "Come here," the toad croaked quietly to the son. "This bird is really a beautiful, young girl. A nasty witch turned her into a bird because she wouldn't marry the witch's horrible son. Now, take her to your father."

The son picked up the bird and the toad, and carried them back to the farmhouse. "This bird is the corn robber," he said to his father. His brothers wanted to kill the bird, but the youngest son said, "No, it's mine and I'm going to keep it."

The next morning, the youngest son carried the bird and the toad back to the well. There, by the well, was a splendid house. At that moment the bird vanished, but the door of the house opened, and a beautiful girl came running out. The son knew that this was his wife and fell in love with her at once.

They were soon married and lived very happily in their new house. The old farmer came to live with them, and the two other sons went off to the city, never to be seen again.

The toad lived by the well. "My father likes to hear your singing. You may sing whenever you like," the youngest son said to it. "Thank you," replied the toad, "I was going to anyway!"

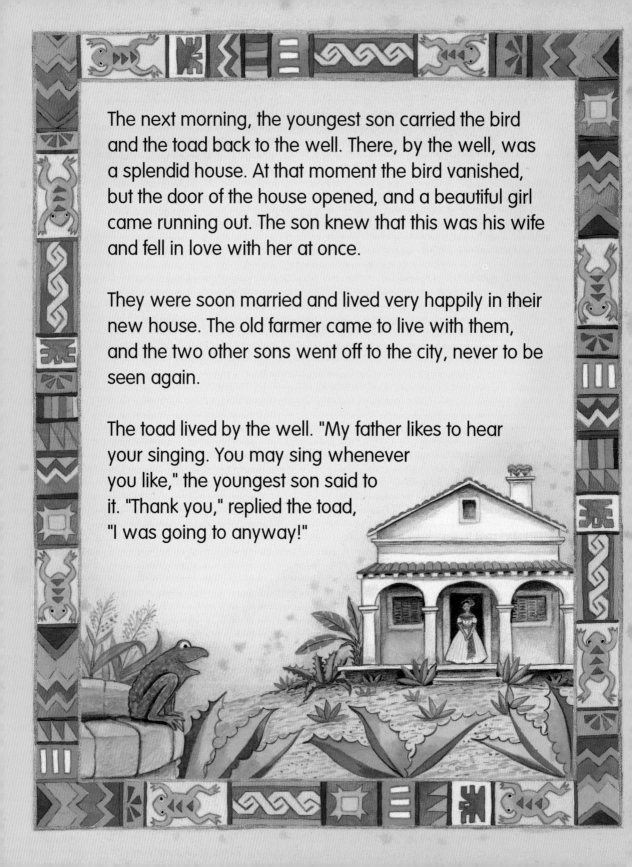

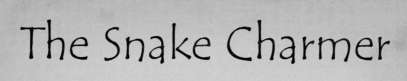

The Snake Charmer

A story from India

Raj lived in a little white house near the Ganges River with his wife, Akba. They were very poor but always happy. Raj earned his living as a snake charmer. Every morning, he would carry a pot with a deadly snake, his mat, and his pipe to the village square. There he would unroll his mat, sit down, take the lid off the pot, and start to play his pipe.

People would come to watch. Slowly the snake would poke its head out of the pot, swaying to the music. Everyone knew that it was a very poisonous snake, so they didn't come too close, but they did throw a few coins to Raj.

At the end of the day, Raj would stop playing.

The snake would disappear into the pot; Raj would put on the lid, roll up his mat, tuck his pipe under his arm, and carry the snake pot home.

One night, after supper, Raj turned to Akba. "Tomorrow I'll walk to the town with my snake. There are more people there than in our village, and they have more money to spend."

The next day, Raj set off at dawn. As soon as he reached the town, he sat down and started to play his pipe. The snake reared out of the pot. A huge crowd gathered around him. They laughed, and cheered and tossed Raj lots of gold coins. He had never seen so much money in his life.

In the evening, Raj collected the gold, picked up the pot, his mat and his pipe, and hurried home.

He didn't see the three robbers watching him. "That snake charmer's got a lot of gold. Let's steal it," growled one, and they followed Raj back to his house.

Raj showed Akba all of the gold he'd been given in the market. She was delighted. "We're rich. Now we'll be able to eat well and I can have a new sari. You're a very clever man," she cried, hugging Raj. She put the gold in a big pot. "Tomorrow, we must find somewhere safe to hide it," she said. She didn't notice the three robbers secretly watching her through the window.

That night, when they were in bed, Akba heard a noise outside the house. "What's that, Raj?" she asked, sitting up. "It's probably only a stray dog. Go to sleep," replied Raj, yawning. "I'm worried about the gold," said Akba. She got out of bed and picked up the pot of gold. Then she looked at the snake pot. "That's just as precious," she said, and carried both pots up to the top of the house where she thought they'd be safe. Then she went back to bed, and to sleep.

Outside the robbers whispered amongst each other. "That silly woman has put the gold upstairs," said one of them. "We'll have to stand on each other's shoulders

54

to get to the window," said another. "I'm the smallest.
I'll climb on top of you two, slip through the window,
and hand down the pot." As quietly as they could, the
robbers carried out their plan. The smallest robber
grabbed the pot, and together they hurried back to
their den.

"We're rich, we're rich," they shouted, dancing around.
One took off the lid of the pot to look at the money.
Instead of gold, a deadly snake slithered out. "Run, run
for your lives," he shouted, and the three robbers were
so frightened, they rushed out of their den and into the
forest, never to be seen again.

In the morning, Raj walked up the stairs to take his
snake to town again. "There's only one pot here," he
called to Akba. "Someone must have stolen the other
one." Akba took the lid off the pot and looked in. It was
full of gold. "They took the wrong pot. What a horrible
surprise for someone," she laughed.

Raj unrolled his mat outside the house, sat down, and
started to play his pipe. After a little while, the snake
came slithering along. Raj picked it up and dropped it
into his pot, all ready for another day's work.

Thor's Hammer

A story from Scandinavia

Thor was the god of thunder. He was a great giant of a god with wild, red hair. When he threw his magic hammer, thunder rolled, lightning flashed, and his hammer flew back to his hand. He loved fighting and feasting, and was always ready for any adventure.

Thor was also the god of law and order. He was usually in a good mood, but he could get angry very quickly. The other gods were very fond of him,

56

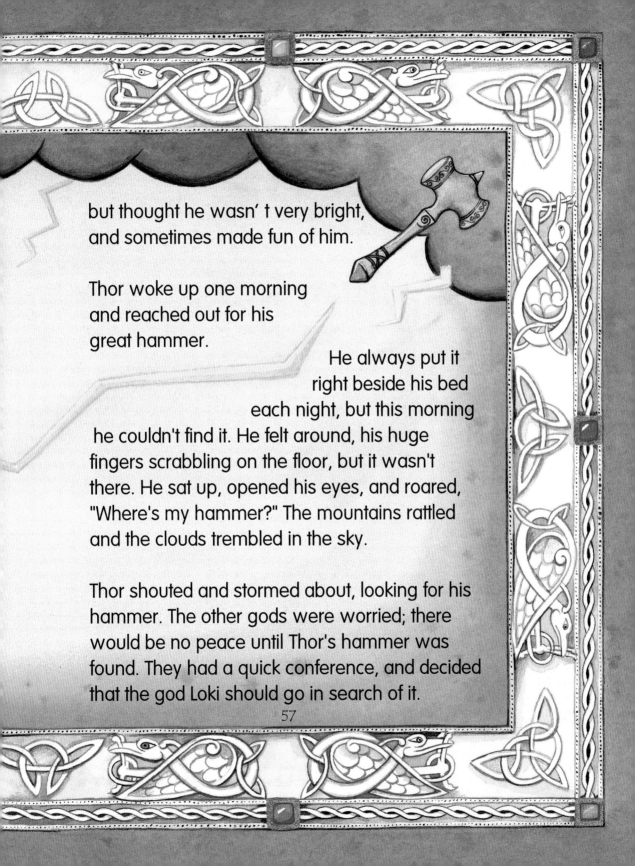

but thought he wasn't very bright, and sometimes made fun of him.

Thor woke up one morning and reached out for his great hammer.

He always put it right beside his bed each night, but this morning he couldn't find it. He felt around, his huge fingers scrabbling on the floor, but it wasn't there. He sat up, opened his eyes, and roared, "Where's my hammer?" The mountains rattled and the clouds trembled in the sky.

Thor shouted and stormed about, looking for his hammer. The other gods were worried; there would be no peace until Thor's hammer was found. They had a quick conference, and decided that the god Loki should go in search of it.

57

Loki went to the beautiful goddess, Freya. He borrowed her magic cloak, and flew swiftly to the Land of the Giants. There, among the mountains covered with ice and snow, he met an enormous frost giant named Thrym. "What are you doing here?" Thrym shouted.

"I'm looking for Thor's hammer. Have you seen it?" asked Loki. Thrym grinned, his beard crackling with ice. "I stole it," he growled. "I've hidden it so deep in the earth, no one will ever find it. I'll only give it back if Freya will marry me."

Loki flew back to Thor and told him the news. Together they went to see Freya. "I'll never marry that horrible giant, Thrym," she screamed furiously. The other gods came to see what the noise was all about. They tried to persuade Freya to marry Thrym, but she just screamed, "No, no, no." Then the god, Heimdall, said, "I've got an idea. We'll dress Thor in a white dress like a

58

bride, and cover his head with a veil. Then he can go to Thrym, pretending to be Freya, and get his hammer back. Simple!"

"What a stupid idea. I won't do it," roared Thor, but the other gods persuaded him to try. They dressed him up so he was covered in beautiful white clothes, veils and precious jewels. Then they dressed Loki up as his maid. Still grumbling, Thor set off with Loki for the Land of the Giants.

Thrym welcomed them and invited them into his huge hall, where a great wedding feast was ready. With great ceremony, Thrym led Thor to the head of the table, and sat beside him. "What would you like to eat, my dear?" he asked. "Perhaps some salmon, and a little slice of roasted ox?"

Thor was hungry. Keeping his face hidden under the veil, he grabbed and ate three whole

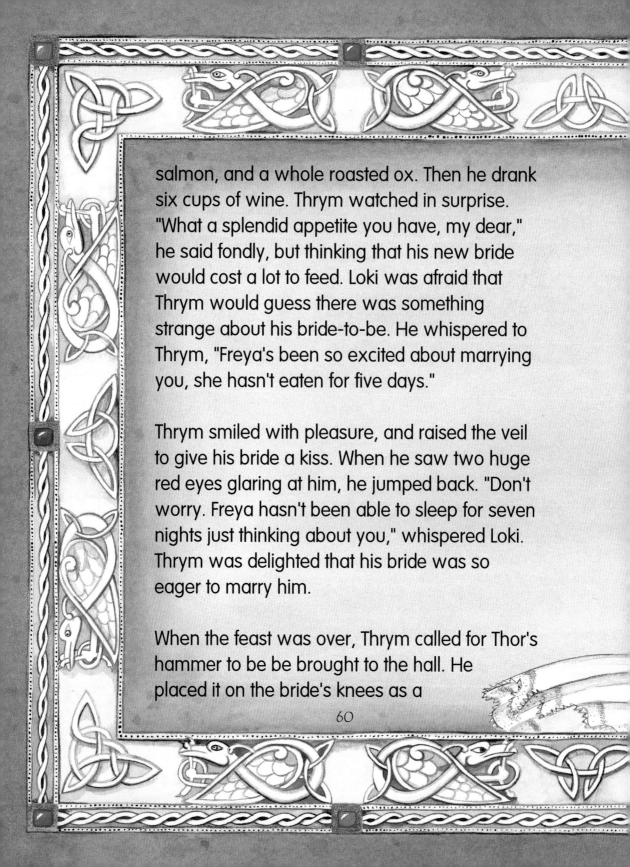

salmon, and a whole roasted ox. Then he drank six cups of wine. Thrym watched in surprise. "What a splendid appetite you have, my dear," he said fondly, but thinking that his new bride would cost a lot to feed. Loki was afraid that Thrym would guess there was something strange about his bride-to-be. He whispered to Thrym, "Freya's been so excited about marrying you, she hasn't eaten for five days."

Thrym smiled with pleasure, and raised the veil to give his bride a kiss. When he saw two huge red eyes glaring at him, he jumped back. "Don't worry. Freya hasn't been able to sleep for seven nights just thinking about you," whispered Loki. Thrym was delighted that his bride was so eager to marry him.

When the feast was over, Thrym called for Thor's hammer to be be brought to the hall. He placed it on the bride's knees as a present. Thor leaped up, threw off his veil, and swinging his hammer around his head, shouted, "I'm Thor and this is my hammer." Then he and Loki fought their way through the astonished giants, and out of the hall.

Laughing that the trick had worked, and trailing his ruined bridal clothes behind him, Thor led Loki back to the other gods. He showed them that he had his precious hammer back, and no one ever dared steal it again.

Buried Treasure

A story from Italy

Gianni pushed open the door of the old farmhouse. "Good evening, Signor Bruno," he called. "Come in, come in, my friend," answered Signor Bruno. "I'm very happy to see you. Sit down, and have a glass of wine."

The two men drank wine, and chatted about the weather, the crops and their families. Then Gianni said, "Signor Bruno, I can see you are worried about something. What is it?"

Signor Bruno sighed. "It's my grandson, Mario," he said. "He's a good lad, but lazy. All day he lies in a hammock and refuses to do a stroke of work. I don't know what to do with him."

Gianni thought for a while. Then he said, "I've got an idea that may solve the problem," and told Signor Bruno his plan. The old grandfather laughed, "It's a good plan. Let's hope it works."

At eleven o'clock the next morning, Gianni strolled up to the farmhouse where Mario lay dozing in the sun in his hammock. "Good morning, Mario," said Gianni, quietly. He pulled a piece of old, crumpled paper out of his pocket, and looked at it.

"I've found this old map," he said. "It's very hard to read, but it seems to say that there are fifty gold pieces buried in that field over there." Mario sat up. "Fifty pieces of gold? I could do with that. Let's go and look for it," he said, and jumped down from the hammock.

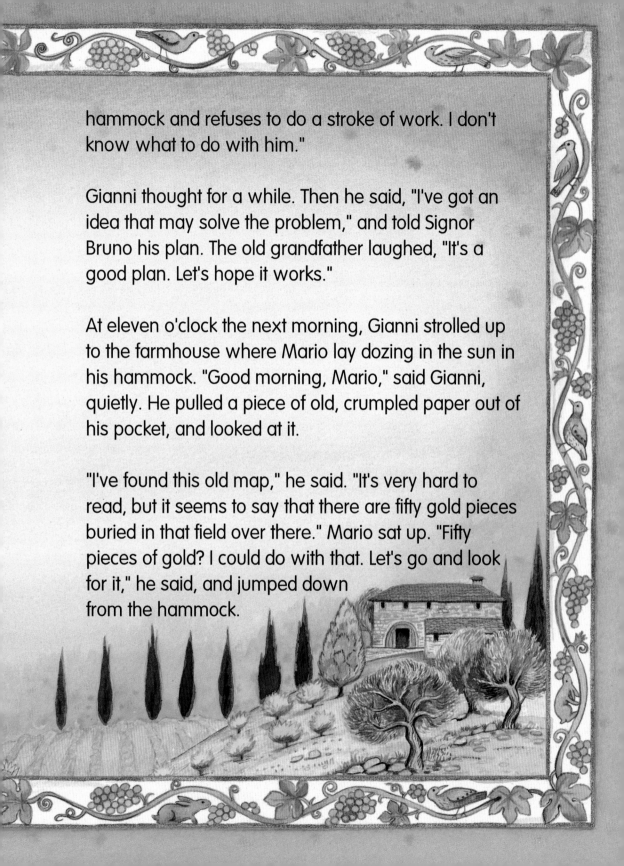

Together, Mario and Gianni hurried to the field, stopped and looked at it. It was covered with tall, thick weeds. "We'll have to clear those weeds before we can start looking for the gold," said Mario, and ran back to the farmhouse to fetch some tools. Then he worked all day, clearing the field of the weeds.

The next morning, Mario was up early, and when Gianni arrived at the field, Mario was busily digging. The soil was so dry that he was throwing up great clouds of dust. "You'll have to water it," said Gianni, and Mario ran off to fetch the hose. Then he watered the whole field.

Gianni took out his map and peered at it. "Perhaps you should start digging for the gold over there," he said, pointing. Just then, a whole troop of chattering children came home from school, and ran across the field. "I'll have to keep them away from here. They might find the gold," said Mario. "I know, I'll cover it with manure. That will keep them off."

He hurried away and fetched a horse and cart. He loaded it with manure from the stables and spread it all over the field. Then he started digging. He began at the north side, then he dug the south side, then the west and finally the east side. Mario dug the whole field, but he didn't find any gold. He was so fed-up that he decided to go back to the farmhouse. He didn' t see Gianni dropping seeds as he walked across the field.

"Maybe I didn' t read the map properly," Gianni said when he joined Mario back at the house. "I'll send the map to a clever friend of mine. He'll be able to read this strange writing. I'll let you know as soon as I hear from him."

Mario waited for weeks and weeks. At last, Gianni came one morning. "Come and look at your field," he said. Together, and with the old grandfather, Signor Bruno, they walked to the field. Mario stared at it in surprise. The whole field was covered with rows and rows of juicy lettuce. "You see what all your clearing, watering, manuring and digging has done," laughed Gianni. "I just planted some seeds for you."

Just then a merchant drove up in his horse and cart. "You can have all of this lettuce for fifty pieces of gold," Signor Bruno called to him. The merchant counted out the gold, and gave it to the old grandfather. Mario and Gianni cut all of the lettuce, and loaded it into the merchant's cart. "Here are your fifty pieces of gold," the grandfather laughed, handing them over to Mario. "They were there in the field all the time. You had to grow them."

Mario stared at his grandfather and then at Gianni. "I think you two planned this," he said, frowning. Then he laughed. He thanked his grandfather for the money, but wanted to give it to Gianni. Gianni wouldn't take it. "It's yours," he said, "you worked for it."

From then on, Mario worked hard on his grandfather's farm, and grew huge crops of wonderful vegetables. And every year, he gave Gianni enough seeds to grow a whole field of lettuce.

Brave Hendrick

A story from Holland

Hendrick hurried out of school and ran along the top of a dyke. (This was one of the great walls which protected the low-lying farmland of Holland from the North Sea.)

Hendrick's father had said to him, "Your grandfather helped to build these dykes. Now I work on them, mending any holes or gaps made by the wind and waves. If the sea broke through, it would drown all the animals, flood our houses, and ruin our farms. We must always watch the dykes."

Hendrick ran on along a dyke he had never explored before. On one side, the tide was creeping in. On the other side was his uncle's farm.

It was very quiet that evening, just the sound of the waves lapping against the dyke. Hendrick was turning around to go home when he heard a noise. He

listened for a moment. He could hear a trickle of water. "I wonder what that is. I'd better have a look," he said to himself.

He scrambled down the dyke and ran along it until he found where the noise was coming from. There was a very small hole in the dyke and the water was trickling through. Hendrick knew that soon the tide would come in and the sea would quickly make the hole bigger and bigger, washing away clay and stones until the water gushed through.

"Help, help," he shouted, but there was no answer. He stared at the hole, wondering what to do. "If I run home and tell my Dad, it may be too late when he gets here, and the water will be roaring through by then," he said to himself. "I must do something."

He looked at the hole and suddenly he had an idea. He pushed in his finger and gasped with relief when no water came out. He had stopped the leak. Leaning against the dyke, he shouted, "Help, help," until he was hoarse.

Hendrick shivered in the wind. His finger in the hole was so cold that he couldn't feel it. It was growing dark, and he could hear the sea thundering against the

other side of the dyke. He was beginning to feel really scared. "Please, please, someone come and help me," he cried.

Hendrick didn't know how long he had been crouching against the dyke. "They must have missed me by now," he said to himself. "They must be looking for me." He thought of his warm, snug house, his mother getting supper and wiped away a few tears. "I'm not going to give up," he said aloud. "I'm nearly ten and I'm not going to give up." Shivering with cold, he wrapped his coat tighter around him.

When it was so dark that Hendrick could only hear the wind howling and the waves dashing against the dyke, he saw a light bobbing along above him. "Help, help me," he croaked. The light stopped and a man with a lantern looked down."Who's there?" he called, climbing down. He held up the lantern and looked at Hendrick. "What's a little lad like you doing out here on the dyke at this time of night?" he growled.

Hendrick, trembling with cold, managed to tell him all about the trickle of water. "Hold on a little longer and I'll soon get help," said the man.

70

At that moment, they heard voices calling along the dyke and could see the lights of lanterns. It was Hendrick's father and uncle, and many men from the village who were out searching for Hendrick.

"Here he is, here's your lad," shouted the man. "I was late coming home from work and found him down by the dyke." The man then told them all about the trickle of water.

"We'll soon fix that," said Hendrick's uncle, and he and the other men set to work at once.

Hendrick's father rushed down the dyke and picked Hendrick up. He wrapped the shivering boy in his coat before carrying him home. "Don't you worry about the dyke any more. It's mended now," he said. "What you need right now is a good hot supper and a warm bed. You're a very brave boy, and I'm proud of you. You did the right thing. You've saved us all from a lot of very bad trouble."

This happened a very long time ago, but in Holland they still tell the story of the brave little boy who kept his finger in the dyke.

Clever Aisha

A story from Morocco

Hassan was a coppersmith who lived in the old city of Marrakesh. He was delighted when his wife gave birth to a girl. They called her Aisha. But Hassan's wife was very ill and, after a few weeks, she died. Heart-broken, Hassan didn't know what to do. He went to work in the morning, leaving Aisha alone in her cradle.

When he came back in the evening, the baby was still asleep in her cradle, but she'd been washed and fed and was happy. Hassan was delighted. This happened again the next day, and the one after that, but Hassan saw nobody. After a while, he began to realize that the jinns (which were kind, invisible spirits) were looking after his daughter for him.

Aisha grew up into a very pretty girl. The jinns taught her all kinds of things, and she became wise and clever. One evening, when Aisha was seventeen, Hassan came home looking very miserable. "What's the matter, Papa?" Aisha asked.

"The Sultan has decided to see how clever his people are," replied Hassan, holding his head in his hands. "He is asking everyone in turn a question. If they can't answer it correctly by the next day, he has their heads chopped off. If they give the right answer, he gives them a bag of gold. Today he asked me 'what does the waterwheel say as it turns?' I can't think of an answer."

"Oh, Papa, that's easy," laughed Aisha. "Now listen carefully, and do exactly as I tell you." She taught Hassan a rhyme, and made him say it over and over again so he wouldn't forget it.

When Hassan went to the Sultan the next morning, he pretended to listen to the waterwheel for a while, and then he said: "I was a quince, I was a tree, the Sultan was hurt, he cut down me."

The Sultan was very surprised that Hassan somehow knew that, many years ago, when the Sultan was walking in his garden, he had hit his head on a quince tree. He had been so angry with the tree that he had cut it down, and had the wood made into the waterwheel. The Sultan was mean and didn't want to give Hassan a bag of gold for getting the answer right so he asked him another riddle.

Again, Hassan went home to Aisha in despair. "What shall I do?" he cried. "The Sultan says that I must go to the palace tomorrow 'riding and walking, laughing and crying, all at the same time'. How can I possibly do that?" Aisha laughed. "That's easy, Papa," and she told him what to do.

The next morning, Hassan rode to the palace on a very small donkey. It was so small that Hassan's feet were on the ground, so he was riding and walking. He knew he looked very funny, so he laughed. Aisha had given him a peeled onion, which he held to his eyes, and that made his eyes stream with tears so he

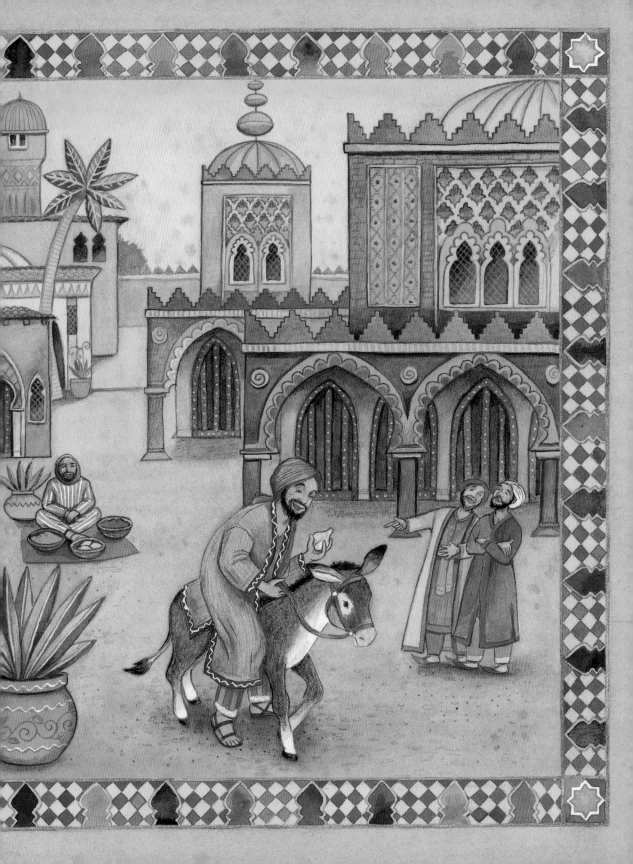

was laughing and crying at the same time. When Hassan reached the palace, he looked so funny that all of the courtiers laughed. The Sultan wasn't pleased but he had to laugh too. "Hassan, you've proved that you are clever. You've earned your bag of gold."

Hassan got off the donkey, and bowed very low. "Sire, I'm an honest man, and I must confess that my daughter, Aisha, told me the answers."

The Sultan frowned for a moment, then he ordered: "Your daughter should be given the bag of gold. Bring her to my palace."

Dressed in her best clothes, Aisha walked with Hassan to the palace. Hassan was terrified, but Aisha was not in the least bit scared. She smiled at the Sultan, and laughed when he growled at her.

The Sultan was enchanted by the pretty, clever girl, and decided to marry her. Over the years, he changed from being a cruel, bad-tempered man into the kindest Sultan his people had ever had.

The Ivory Wand

A story from China

Wang-Su lived in the city of Nanjing. A high wall with a locked gate surrounded his house. Every day the old man opened his gate and walked out, carefully closing it behind him. Then he strolled through the streets, his cat stepping ahead of him, and his big dog plodding by his side.

The people who lived near Wang-Su were puzzled. They could see the old man was richly dressed, the cat was sleek, and the dog well-fed, but he never went to the market, or the stores. He never bought anything. "Where," they wondered, "does he get his food and his clothes?"

One evening, a robber climbed over the wall of

Wang-Su's garden, and crept up to the house. Peering through a window, he saw the old man sitting at a table in a room full of fine furniture, silk hangings, and beautiful carpets. The old man picked up a little ivory wand, and turned to the cat.

"I know what you would like," he said, and waved his wand. At once, a big plate of fish appeared. Then he said to the dog, "I know what you would like," and waved his wand. Immediately, a big bowl full of juicy meat appeared. Then he said, "I know what I would like," waved his wand, and all sorts of delicious foods appeared on the table.

The robber hid in the garden until Wang-Su, the cat and the dog were in bed, and fast asleep. Then he crept into the house, and stole the little ivory wand. When Wang-Su woke the next morning, and couldn't find his ivory wand anywhere, he knew it had been stolen. "What shall I do now?" he asked the cat and the dog. "Without my wand, we shall all starve to death."

Hungry and sad, the cat and the dog wandered out into the garden. "We must find the ivory wand and bring it back to our dear master," meowed the cat. "Let's go at once," growled the dog, and together they leaped over the wall, and started on their search.

Day after day, they searched all of the streets of the city, but there was no sign of the ivory wand anywhere. After many months, they came to a very grand house. "This is the place," growled the dog. "I can smell it."

The cat and dog ran quickly past the guards at the door of the house, and out into the garden. There, under a cherry tree, stood the robber, dressed in the most magnificent clothes. On a chain around his neck was the ivory wand. The dog barked furiously at the robber, and jumped at him, knocking him down. The cat sprang onto his shoulder, gripped the ivory wand in her jaws, and pulled until the chain broke. "Run, run as fast as you can," meowed the cat to the dog. Dodging the guards, they scampered out of the house, and away down the street. The guards shouted and waved sticks, chasing them, but the cat and the dog soon lost them in the narrow alleyways.

Tired and panting, they found their way back to Wang-Su's house. The gate in the wall was open, and the garden was a mass of weeds. In the house, Wang-Su sat in an empty room, dressed in rags. When he saw the cat and the dog, he cried, "Oh my dear friends, you've come back to me. I've been so lonely without you, and I've had to sell everything I own." The cat jumped up on his lap and dropped the ivory wand into his hand. The dog rested his head on the old man's knee, and licked his other hand.

"You clever, clever friends," laughed Wang-Su, stroking the cat and patting the dog. Waving his ivory wand, the old man fed the cat and the dog with all the food they liked best, and then he had a delicious meal too. Soon the house and the garden looked beautiful again,

and Wang-Su strolled out every day with his cat and his dog. The people were pleased to see him in the streets again, but they never discovered the secret of his little ivory wand.

Nail Soup

A story from the Czech Republic

Long ago, a cold, tired and hungry man trudged down a dusty country road. He shivered as the wind blew through the tatters in his coat. Pushing his hands deep into his pockets, he carefully searched them for a coin, but all he found was a big rusty nail.

When he reached a village, he knocked on the door of the first house that he came to, but no one answered. He knocked again, louder this time. At last, he heard the sound of a key in the lock and some bolts being drawn back. The door opened a few inches and a mean old woman peered out.

"Good evening, Madam," said the man, "I wonder if

you could spare a cold, hungry man a bite to eat." The old woman opened the door a little wider. "I' ve no food in the house," she croaked, "but you can come in for a few minutes and warm yourself."

Soon the man was sitting by a roaring fire with the old woman sitting opposite him. She said nothing. After a while, the man took the big rusty nail from his pocket, wiped it on his sleeve, and tossed it from hand to hand. When he was sure the old woman was watching, he said, "Yesterday I had the best soup I've ever eaten made with just this old nail."

"What a load of nonsense! You can't make soup with a nail," cackled the old woman. "If you had such a thing as a big pot of water, I could prove it to you," answered the man.

Grumbling, the old woman fetched a big pot, and put it on the stove. When the water was boiling, the man dropped in the nail. After waiting ten minutes, he picked up the spoon, and tasted the water.

"Delicious," he said, "but I think it could do with just a little pepper and salt, if you have them."

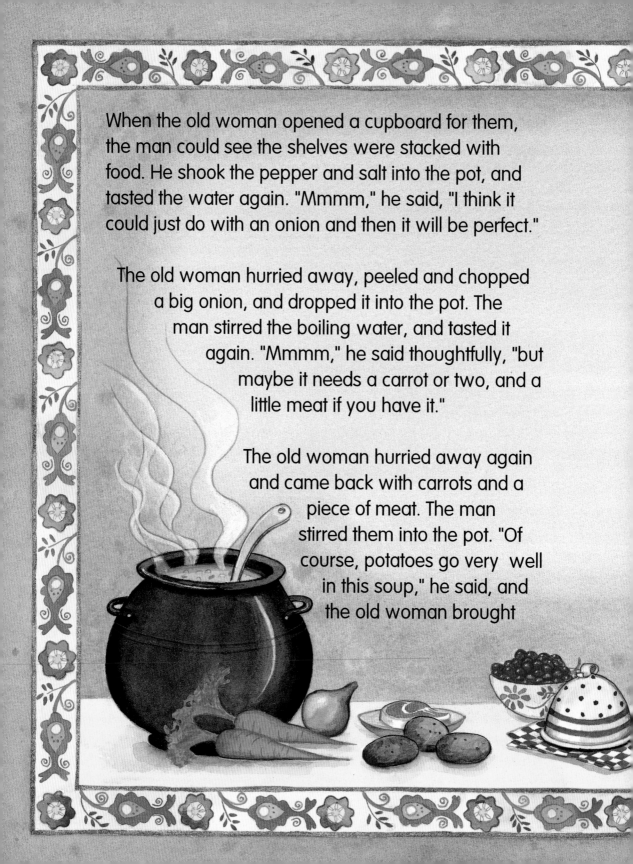

When the old woman opened a cupboard for them, the man could see the shelves were stacked with food. He shook the pepper and salt into the pot, and tasted the water again. "Mmmm," he said, "I think it could just do with an onion and then it will be perfect."

The old woman hurried away, peeled and chopped a big onion, and dropped it into the pot. The man stirred the boiling water, and tasted it again. "Mmmm," he said thoughtfully, "but maybe it needs a carrot or two, and a little meat if you have it."

The old woman hurried away again and came back with carrots and a piece of meat. The man stirred them into the pot. "Of course, potatoes go very well in this soup," he said, and the old woman brought potatoes, peeled and cut into chunks. The man dropped them in, and sat down by the fire. "Not long now," he said, "and doesn' t it smell good?"

After half-an-hour, he tasted the soup again, and said, "That's perfect now. I hope, Madam, you will join me in eating this soup."

Almost smiling, the old woman laid the table with a cloth and her best china. The man poured the soup into two big bowls and sat down at the table with the old woman. He dipped his spoon into the soup and then stopped.

"You've been so kind, I wish I had some wine for you to drink with the soup," he said. "I think I've a bottle somewhere," said the old woman, and soon came back with the wine and two glasses.

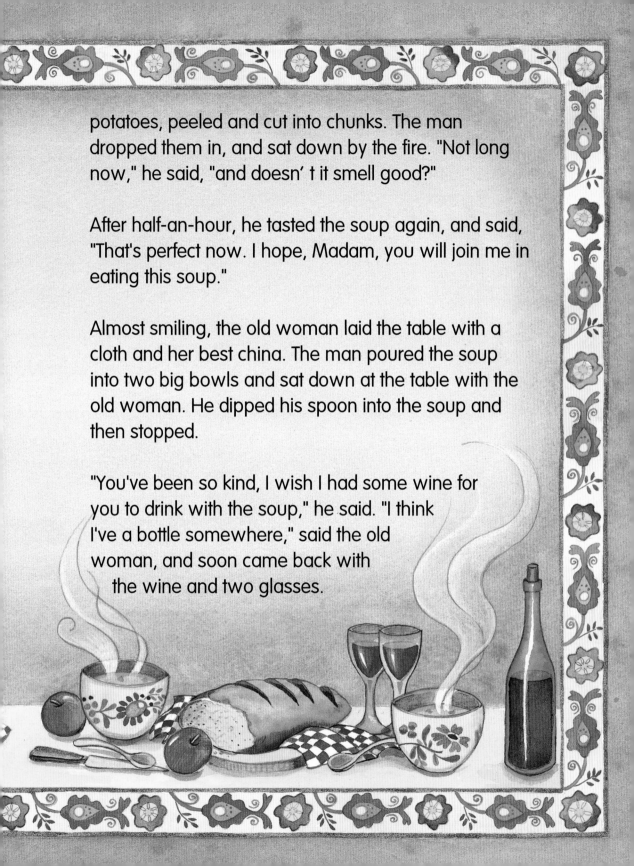

While the man and the old woman ate the soup, and drank the wine, they talked and talked. The old woman brought out a crusty loaf of bread, cheese, fruit and a big cake. They told each other stories, laughed a lot and had a merry evening. The old woman couldn't remember when she had enjoyed herself so much.

When they had eaten all they could, and were growing sleepy, the old woman said, "It's getting late. I'll make up the bed in the spare room for you. You'll be warm and comfortable in there." The man thanked her, and when she was out of the room, he scooped the nail from the bottom of the soup pot, wiped it and dropped it into his pocket.

Next morning, the man thanked the old woman again. "I'd never have believed you could make such good soup with just an old nail," she said.

The man smiled, and murmured, "It's what you add to it that makes all the difference." Then he patted his pocket to make sure the nail was there. "I may need that again tonight," he said quietly to himself as he walked away down the road.

The Four Brothers

A story from Spain

A farmer who lived in the mountains of Spain had four sons. They were called Alfredo, Bernardo, Ernesto, and Pedro. (Please try to remember their names.) Alfredo, Bernardo and Ernesto didn't like living on the farm. They said working in the fields was too much like hard work, looking after the sheep was boring, and milking the goats was messy. Pedro loved farm work. He sang while he was in the fields, he whistled when he looked after the sheep and he hummed while he milked the goats.

One day, Alfredo said, "We've decided that it's time we four brothers went out into the big wide world to seek our fortunes." "Thank you, but I'd rather stay at home," said Pedro. "Well you can't," said Alfredo.

The father was very sad, but he went to his money box and counted out all the money he had. He gave one silver peso to each of his sons, hugged them, and sent them on their way. Alfredo, Bernardo and Ernesto had to drag Pedro along the road. When they came to a crossroads, they stopped. "Which way shall we go?" asked Bernardo. "I'll go along the north road, you can go along the south one, Ernesto will go east, and Pedro can follow the west road," said Alfredo. "Thank you, but I'd rather go home," said Pedro.

"In a year and a day, we'll all meet here, and then we'll have an adventure," said Alfredo. The four brothers said, "Goodbye and good luck". They made Pedro walk along the west road, and set off along their own roads.

Alfredo walked for an hour or two when, suddenly, he was surrounded by a band of robbers. They stole his silver peso and beat him. "You come with us," one growled, dragging him to their home in the mountains. Alfredo soon proved to be so brave that the robbers made him their leader. "It's a great life," he thought, "I can steal anything I want. I'm going to be rich."

Bernardo hurried along his road until he met a man carrying a gun. Bernardo persuaded the man to sell him the gun for one silver peso. In the woods, Bernardo fired his gun again and again, until he became so good, he could shoot one leaf off a tree at a tremendous distance. When he came to a village, he won so many prizes at shooting matches, he grew very rich.

Ernesto strolled along the east road and there he met a man who was gazing around him through very strange spectacles. "What are you doing?" said Ernesto.

"With these glasses, I can see what's going on all over the world," said the man. "Why, there's the Emperor of China drinking tea, and that must be the Shah of Persia riding his great, white stallion." Ernesto persuaded the man to sell him the glasses for one silver peso, and then he walked on to the nearest town. There people paid him lots of money to tell them what was happening in the world.

Pedro trudged along his road until he came to a blacksmith. Pedro stopped to watch him mending pots and pans, and all sorts of things. "That's a useful trade. Will you teach me how to do it for one silver peso?" asked Pedro. The blacksmith agreed, and set Pedro to work. Pedro didn't earn much money, but he became very good at mending anything that was broken.

After a year and a day, the four brothers met at the crossroads and told each other all that they had done. "Now we'll have an adventure," said Alfredo. "Thank you, but I'd rather go home," said Pedro.

Ernesto put on his spectacles. "I can see a Princess locked up in a tower on an island. The island is guarded by a fierce sea monster. Her father, the King, has decreed that whoever rescues the Princess may marry her."

"That's a very good adventure," said Alfredo. " Let's rescue the Princess, and one of us will marry her." "Thank you, but I'd rather go home," said Pedro.

Alfredo, Bernardo and Ernesto marched Pedro along the road, over the mountains, through the forests until, at last, they came to the seashore. There, they found a ship that they could sail to the Princess's island. "We'll wait until it's dark, and the sea monster is asleep," said Alfredo.

Just after midnight, the four brothers sailed the ship out to the island and landed quietly on the shore. They tiptoed right up to the tower, gently woke up the

Princess and led her down to the ship. They helped her aboard and were just pushing the ship away from the shore when Ernesto stepped on the sea monster's tail. It woke up with a great roar, and chased the ship as it sailed away. Quickly loading his gun, Bernardo shot the sea monster, but as it died, its lashing tail smashed a hole in the ship. Pedro snatched up his tools and mended the ship, which sailed safely back to the shore.

The four brothers took the Princess to the King, and told him how they had rescued her. He was delighted to have his daughter brought safely home. "Now, which one of you is going to marry her?" he asked.

"I am. I stole her away," said Alfredo. "I shot the sea monster which would have killed us," said Bernardo. "I saw the Princess on the island in the first place," said Ernesto. "And what did you do?" the King asked Pedro. "I mended the ship when it was about to sink and drown us all," replied Pedro. "Then you shall marry my daughter and live in my palace," commanded the King, and the three brothers didn't dare argue with him.

Pedro bowed politely. "Thank you, but I'd rather go home," he said. The Princess laughed. "I've always wanted to marry a farmer," she cried. She ran to Pedro and, hand in hand, they walked down the road, talking and laughing all the way home.

Stealing the Sun

A story from Africa

Chief Wai lived near Lake Tumba with his wives and many servants. He had a tall, handsome young son, named Mokele. At that time there was no sun, only dull, overcast skies all day and the bright moon at night. One day, Mokele asked his father, "Why doesn't the sun shine here?" Chief Wai looked sad. "It was stolen away a very long time ago."

"I'll go and get the sun back for you," said Mokele.

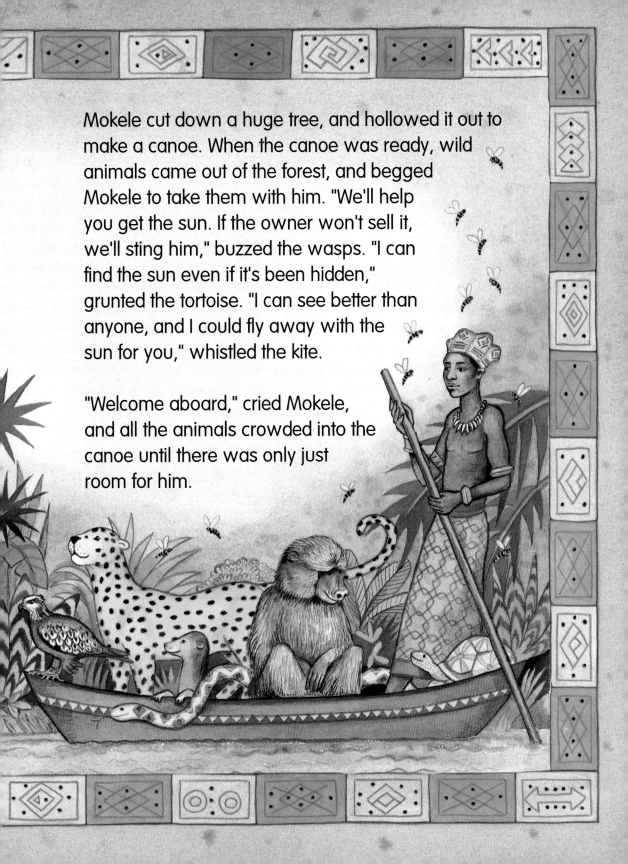

Mokele cut down a huge tree, and hollowed it out to make a canoe. When the canoe was ready, wild animals came out of the forest, and begged Mokele to take them with him. "We'll help you get the sun. If the owner won't sell it, we'll sting him," buzzed the wasps. "I can find the sun even if it's been hidden," grunted the tortoise. "I can see better than anyone, and I could fly away with the sun for you," whistled the kite.

"Welcome aboard," cried Mokele, and all the animals crowded into the canoe until there was only just room for him.

For days, Mokele paddled along the rivers through the forests until, at last, he came to the land of Chief Mokulaka, who had hidden the sun. Mokele asked him, very politely, "Please may I buy the sun from you?" Chief Mokulaka didn't want to sell the sun, but when he saw a fierce leopard, a huge baboon, and all the other animals that were in the canoe, he knew it would be difficult to keep it.

"Very well," he said, "but I'll have to talk to my son to decide on a fair price. Why not go and rest for a while?" Mokele agreed, and sat down under a tree. Chief Mokulaka hurried to his daughter. "Molumba," he whispered, "I want to kill this man. Brew up some poison for him." The Chief didn't notice the wasp that was hovering near them. The wasp flew to Mokele, and warned him what the Chief was planning.

When the Chief invited Mokele into Molumba's hut, Mokele pretended he knew nothing of the poison. He talked to Molumba, and she so liked this handsome young man, she secretly poured the poison away.

While they were talking, the tortoise found the sun hidden in a cave. It dragged it out and held it tightly.

The kite gripped the tortoise in its claws, and lifted it up. For the first time, the sun rose up in the sky. When Mokele and the animals saw the sun shining over the forest, they rushed to the canoe, and Molumba went with them. Mokele paddled as fast as he could away down the river. Shouting with rage, Chief Mokulaka and his warriors chased after them, but a huge swarm of wasps stung them until they ran away.

Mokele paddled his canoe
back to his village. "Father,"
he shouted, "I've brought
the sun for you." His father
and all the people cheered.
They were delighted the sun
was going to rise again every
morning, lighting up the forest,
and making the days bright.

Mokele married Molumba, and they were very happy.
Mokele told the story of his adventure over and over
again. He told his children, and his grandchildren, and
the people who live in the forest are still telling the story
of how Mokele brought back the sun.

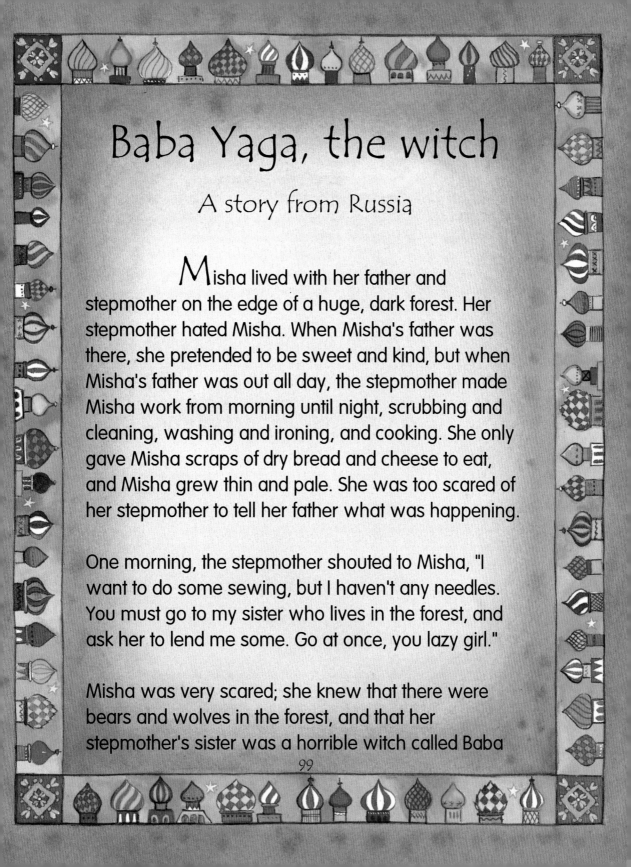

Baba Yaga, the witch

A story from Russia

Misha lived with her father and stepmother on the edge of a huge, dark forest. Her stepmother hated Misha. When Misha's father was there, she pretended to be sweet and kind, but when Misha's father was out all day, the stepmother made Misha work from morning until night, scrubbing and cleaning, washing and ironing, and cooking. She only gave Misha scraps of dry bread and cheese to eat, and Misha grew thin and pale. She was too scared of her stepmother to tell her father what was happening.

One morning, the stepmother shouted to Misha, "I want to do some sewing, but I haven't any needles. You must go to my sister who lives in the forest, and ask her to lend me some. Go at once, you lazy girl."

Misha was very scared; she knew that there were bears and wolves in the forest, and that her stepmother's sister was a horrible witch called Baba

Yaga. Baba Yaga was very ugly, and had iron teeth. But Misha did as she was told. When her stepmother wasn't looking, she took a piece of cheese and a bone with a little meat, and tied them up in a handkerchief. Then she began to walk down the path to the forest.

At last, Misha came to a clearing in the forest. Inside a fence was a little house. Misha opened the gate, and stepped inside. A very thin dog came growling and barking at her. "Poor thing," she said. "You look half-starved." Quickly she untied her handkerchief, and gave the dog the bone. She patted its head, and it looked up at her with its huge, dark eyes.

Misha walked to the little house and pushed open the door. A very thin cat, snarling and spitting, leaped at her. "Poor thing," said Misha, "you look half-starved," and she gave the cat the piece of cheese. The cat purred when Misha stroked its back.

"Baba Yaga is out, but she'll soon be back. Go while you still have a chance or she'll eat you for supper," meowed the cat. But before Misha could reach the door, she heard a swishing noise. She peeked through a window and there she saw Baba Yaga in a huge

100

mortar, steering with a pestle, just landing outside the fence. Baba Yaga climbed out, came crashing through the door, and stopped when she saw Misha. "What do you want?" she screeched. Misha was almost too frightened to speak, but she managed to say, "Your sister sent me to borrow some needles."

"Did she? Did she indeed?" cackled Baba Yaga. "Well, you'll have to wait until after supper. First, I'm going to have a bath," she croaked, gnashing her iron teeth. "You can do some weaving while you're waiting," and she went into the bathhouse, slamming the door.

"Quick Misha, go now," meowed the cat, "or you'll never escape. Take the needles; I'll do the weaving so Baba Yaga will hear the loom clacking away, and think you're working it. Take this towel, and this comb. When

Baba Yaga comes after you, throw down the towel first and then the comb. Now go."

"Thank you, thank you," whispered Misha and tiptoed to the door. She hurried down the steps. The dog ran up to her, but it didn't bark. Misha ran away down the path through the forest as fast as she could.

In the little house, Baba Yaga, shouted from the bathhouse, "Are you weaving, my dear?" The cat worked the loom, clackety-clack, clackety-clack. "Yes, Auntie," she meowed, trying to sound like Misha.

When Baba Yaga came out of the bathhouse, she saw the cat sitting at the loom, and screamed, "Why did you let that girl escape? You should have warned me." The cat stared at Baba Yaga. "I've worked for you for years and years, but you never gave me a piece of cheese like she did," she meowed. Baba Yaga tried to kick the cat, but the cat jumped out of the window, and disappeared into the forest.

Gnashing her iron teeth with rage, Baba Yaga ran out of the cottage. When she saw the dog, she shrieked, "Why didn't you bark to warn me that girl was getting

away?" The dog looked at her. "I've worked for you for years and years but you never gave me anything. Misha was kind to me and gave me a bone with meat on it." Before Baba Yaga could kick him, the dog leaped over the fence and disappeared into the forest. "I'll get her, I'll get her. She won't escape from me," screamed Baba Yaga, climbing into her mortar. Waving the pestle, she bumped along the path through the forest.

Running as fast as she could, Misha heard the mortar come bumping after her. When it had almost caught up with her, she threw down the towel the cat had given her. At once, a great, wide river flowed between her and Baba Yaga. Baba Yaga landed on the bank, screaming with anger. Her mortar was too heavy to float across the river. She turned the mortar around, and went back to her house. Then she drove her herd of cows to the river where they drank up all the water, and Baba Yaga bumped over the dry riverbed.

When Misha heard the mortar bumping on the path behind her again, she threw down the comb. At once, a thorn forest sprang up. It was so thick, nothing could get through it. Baba Yaga jumped out of her mortar,

and tried to chew the trees down with her iron teeth, but she couldn't do it. Screaming with fury, she jumped back into her mortar and set off back to her house in the forest.

Misha ran on and on, panting and gasping, until she could run no more. Wearily, she stumbled along the path and out of the forest until she could see the lights of her house gleaming in the dark. Her father was standing outside, waiting for her.

"Where have you been?" he asked, hugging her. "I was so worried about you." Through her tears, Misha told him all about Baba Yaga, and everything that had happened to her. "Come in, come in," said her father. "Don't be frightened any more. I didn't know what a horrible woman your stepmother was, but I'll soon see that she gets what she deserves."

Through the window, the stepmother saw Misha with her father. She quickly opened the back door, and ran out into the forest. From then on, Misha lived very happily with her father in the house near the forest. No one knows what happened to the horrible stepmother. She may have gone to stay with Baba Yaga, or she may have been killed by a bear or a wolf in the forest, but she was never, ever seen again.

Dick Whittington

A story from Britain

Dick Whittington was a poor boy who
lived in a small village in Gloucestershire. He had no
mother or father, his clothes were rags, and he ate the
scraps of food anyone would give him. When he was
fourteen, he decided to seek his fortune. He'd heard
that the streets of London were paved with gold, and
there he went to find it.

When, tired and hungry, he reached the great city,
he soon found that there was no gold, only dirty
cobblestones. For days, Dick tried to find work and
somewhere to sleep, but no one took any
notice of the thin, ragged boy.

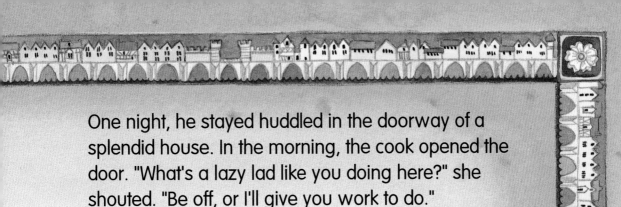

One night, he stayed huddled in the doorway of a splendid house. In the morning, the cook opened the door. "What's a lazy lad like you doing here?" she shouted. "Be off, or I'll give you work to do."

"I'll do anything for a breakfast," said Dick, very cold and hungry. The cook dragged him into the kitchen and set him to work - cleaning pots and pans, scrubbing the floors, running errands, carrying in the coal, and lots of other dirty jobs. He was busy from early morning until late at night, and if he stopped for a moment, the cook beat him with her rolling pin. She would give him only leftover, stale food.

Dick slept in a cold attic on a hard bed with a thin blanket. The attic was home to lots of mice, and their squeakings and scratchings kept him awake. "I'll have to get a cat," thought

Dick, and so he bought one with the first few pennies he earned. After that, it was very quiet in the attic, and Dick slept well.

The owner of the house was a rich merchant named Sir Hugh Fitzwarren. He was a kind and generous man. His young daughter, Alice, often slipped down to the kitchen, and chatted with Dick when the cook was resting in the afternoons. Dick told her all about his village, and how he had come to London. Alice smuggled extra food to him when she could. Dick was very happy to have someone to talk to, and he and Alice became good friends.

One day, all the servants were talking and chattering excitedly about the ship that Sir Hugh was sending to Africa. "The servants can put anything they have to sell on it and when the ship sails back, the captain gives them the money," Alice explained to Dick. "What do you have to sell?"

Dick thought for a moment. "I don't have anything in the world, except my cat," he said. "Well," said Alice. "You must send your cat. It might bring you a few pennies." Dick didn't

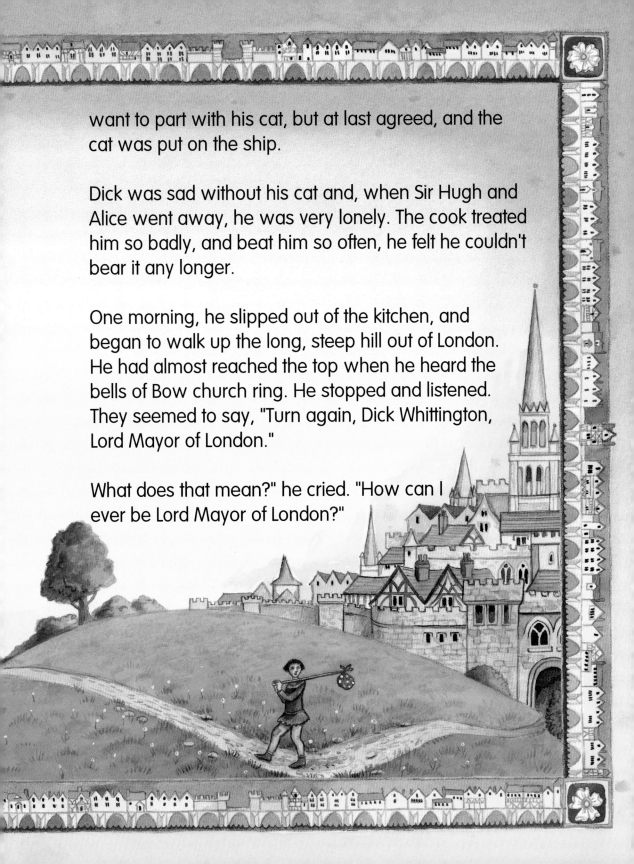

want to part with his cat, but at last agreed, and the cat was put on the ship.

Dick was sad without his cat and, when Sir Hugh and Alice went away, he was very lonely. The cook treated him so badly, and beat him so often, he felt he couldn't bear it any longer.

One morning, he slipped out of the kitchen, and began to walk up the long, steep hill out of London. He had almost reached the top when he heard the bells of Bow church ring. He stopped and listened. They seemed to say, "Turn again, Dick Whittington, Lord Mayor of London."

What does that mean?" he cried. "How can I ever be Lord Mayor of London?"

Puzzled, he turned around, and began the long walk back to London.

When Sir Hugh's ship reached Africa, the captain went at once to the King with the things he had to sell, but left Dick's cat on board. The King was pleased, and paid the captain well. Just as the captain was leaving the King's palace, he noticed there were rats and mice running around everywhere.

"Your Majesty," said the Captain. "I have an animal on my ship that can get rid of all these rats and mice." The King had never heard of such an animal as a cat, but he ordered the captain to bring it immediately.

As soon as the captain put the cat down on the floor of the palace, it killed seven mice, four rats and chased the others away. The King was delighted. "I will buy this wonderful creature. Name your price." The captain thought quickly. "Ten bags of gold," he said. "I'll give you twenty, and this jewel," laughed the King.

When the ship returned to London, the captain took the money to Sir Hugh, who gave the servants what they had earned. Then he called for Dick, but Dick was nowhere to be found. Sir Hugh called for the cook. "He's run away. He's a bad boy, never did a good day's work," she lied. "Oh, Papa," cried Alice. "I know that's not true. We must find Dick at once."

Sir Hugh searched the streets of London until he found Dick, staring hungrily at a baker's shop. "Come with me, my boy," he said smiling, and he took Dick back to his house. "See what your cat has brought you." Dick's eyes grew bigger and bigger as he looked at the twenty bags of gold and the precious jewel. "If you spend it wisely," said Sir Hugh, "you'll be a rich man one day."

Over the next few years, Sir Hugh helped Dick to become a merchant, to buy a splendid house, and was very happy when Dick asked Sir Hugh if he might marry Alice.

Dick did become very rich, but he never forgot what it was like to be poor. He spent some of his great fortune on restoring a London hospital, founding a college, and building almshouses for the old and poor. And he became Sir Richard Whittington, Lord Mayor of London, just as the Bow church bells had told him.

The Magic Doll

A story from North America

Wasis lived with his mother and father, and his six brothers in a great forest. Wasis was the youngest, but he could run faster, shoot further and hunt better than any of his brothers. They were very jealous of him, and often played nasty tricks on him. Wasis grew more and more miserable. "It's no good," he thought, "I'll have to go and find somewhere else to live."

His mother guessed his plan, and although she didn't want him to leave, she made him a lovely pair of moccasins out of the best leather and with the finest stitching. Wasis put them on - they were perfect. He kissed his mother goodbye, and sadly walked away through the forest.

Wasis didn't know that the great god Glooskap was watching him. Glooskap decided to test the boy. He disguised himself as an old man, and appeared on the path ahead of Wasis. When Wasis was about to reach him, the old man dropped a very small, wooden box on the path.

Wasis stopped and picked up the box. For a moment he was tempted to open it, or to slip it into his pocket, but he ran on after the old man. "Grandfather," he called, "you dropped this," and gave the old man the box. "Thank you, thank you, my boy," said the old man. "Can you tell me, please Grandfather, where this path goes?" asked Wasis.

"It leads to a village," answered the old man, "but the way is very rough." Wasis looked down at the old man's bare feet; they were cut by sharp stones and thorns. Wasis took off his lovely new moccasins, and handed them to the old man. "Take these, Grandfather," he said. The old man smiled, and put them on.

Wasis was just about to run on along the path when the old man said, "Take this box, and look after it well." Then he disappeared. Wasis felt quite scared. "That man was magic," he thought. Then he opened the box. Inside was a little doll made of grass. "Oh, but I don't play with dolls," he said, feeling very disappointed. "I'll do whatever you command me," squeaked the doll. Wasis was so surprised he almost dropped the box. He didn't know what to do, so he carefully tucked the box away in his pocket, and ran on along the path through the forest.

When Wasis reached the village, the people greeted him. "Our Chief is out hunting, but come to his tepee," they said. In the tepee sat the Chief's beautiful young

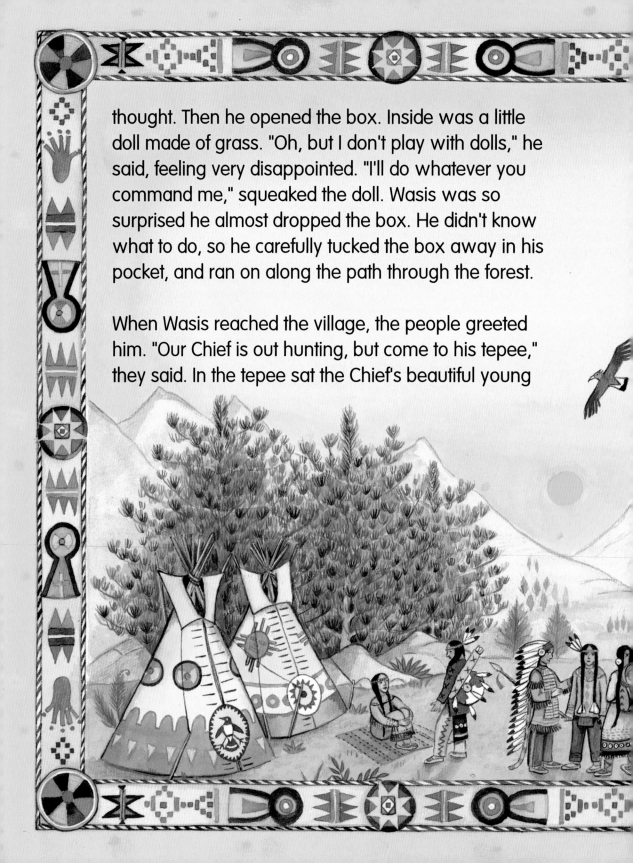

daughter, Seboosis. She gave Wasis food and water, and talked to him while he ate. When the Chief came back from his hunt, he welcomed Wasis, but he wasn't pleased to see how friendly Seboosis was being to the stranger. He could see that Wasis had fallen in love with his daughter, but he wanted Seboosis to marry a young man from their village tribe.

Wasis stayed in the village, hunting with the young men, and talking to Seboosis whenever he could. One day, he asked the Chief, "Please may I marry your daughter? I love her, and I think she loves me."

The Chief frowned, and thought for a moment. Then he said, "You may marry Seboosis if you move that mountain over there. It's in the way of my hunting path." He smiled, quite sure that he had set Wasis an impossible task.

That night, Wasis crept out of his tepee when everyone was asleep. He opened the box, and whispered to the little grass doll, "Move that mountain for me." Then he went back to bed, and to sleep.

In the morning, the Chief stumbled out of his tepee, stretched, and rubbed his eyes. Then he looked all around, and gasped. The mountain had vanished. His hunting path ran straight through the trees. He scowled with anger. "There's magic here," he thought. "No one could move a mountain without it."

When the Chief saw Wasis, he greeted him and pretended to be friendly. "Well done, my boy," he said, "but I've another task for you before you marry Seboosis. On the other side of the lake is a fierce tribe of warriors who are always making war. I want you to go across the lake, and fight them." Wasis said nothing. He walked down to the lake, climbed aboard

a canoe, and paddled away, watched by the whole village. Seboosis was there, trying to hide her tears.

All that day, the people in the village watched and listened. They could hear the noise of a terrible battle going on at the other side of the lake. Then, in the evening, all was silent. They waited until it was dark, but no canoe came back across the lake. They were sure Wasis was dead.

The next day, the Chief had a wedding feast prepared for Seboosis to marry a young man of the tribe. Seboosis was dressed in her wedding clothes, but her eyes were red with tears. When everything was ready, the Chief called, "Let the bridegroom come forth."

"I am here," said Wasis quietly, stepping out of the forest. He walked up to Seboosis, took her hand, and smiled at her. She was overjoyed to see him, alive and well. The Chief was very angry, but he had to let the wedding go on. So Wasis married Seboosis, and they were very happy together. When the Chief died, Wasis was made the Chief of the tribe, and he ruled wisely, but he never asked the magic doll in the box for anything ever again.

The Little Sparrow

A story from Japan

Long ago in Japan there was a kind old man who had a very mean and bad-tempered wife. They had no children but the old man had one pet - a tiny sparrow - that he loved and cared for. Every day, when he came home from work, he talked to the sparrow, stroked its feathers, and fed it with tiny bits of food from his supper plate.

The old man's wife loved and cared for no one, and she particularly hated the sparrow. She hated it living in the house and she was furious that her husband was so fond of it.

One day, when her husband had gone to work, she began to get things ready to wash. She brought out some clothes and a blanket, and then went back for another bundle. When she came back, she saw the sparrow pecking at the blanket. She was so

angry that she grabbed a pair of scissors and snipped off the sparrow's tail. Then she threw it out of the door, shouting, "Go away, you filthy bird, and never come back." The poor little sparrow flipped and flapped away to the woods; flying was very difficult without a proper tail.

When the old man came home for his supper, he couldn't find his sparrow. He looked everywhere, and asked his wife again and again where it was. At last, she told him what she had done. The old man was very upset and went sadly to bed.

The next morning, he searched through the woods, calling and calling for his little sparrow. Suddenly, it came flying to him, wearing a beautiful Japanese dress. "My dear friend," said the sparrow, "you must be tired and hungry. Please come to my house for a rest and some food."

He followed the bird through the woods to a lovely house. There the sparrow's daughters brought the old man delicious things to eat and drink, and four of them did a little dance for him. Finally, he noticed that it was evening. "It's getting late, I must go home," he said.

The sparrow begged him to stay but he said his wife would be worrying about him.

"If you must go, let me give you a present to take with you," said the sparrow, and brought out two baskets.

One was big and heavy, and the other was small and light. "Choose which one you would like," said the bird. The old man didn't want to be greedy, so he picked up the small basket. "I'd like this one, thank you," he said, and walked away through the woods to his house.

When he reached home, he told his wife all about the sparrow. "Quick, let's look in the basket," she said.

Opening the lid, she stopped, gasping with surprise. The basket was full of gold and sparkling jewels, and bags of money. "We'll be rich for the rest of our lives," she cried, and she almost smiled. Then she frowned at the old man, and shouted, "You silly old fool. You should have chosen the big basket. Then we would have

been even richer. I'll go to the sparrow's house tomorrow and get the other basket."

"Please don't," begged the old man. "We already have far more than we need." But the old woman wouldn't listen. The next morning, she walked as fast as she could through the woods until she came to the sparrow's house. "My dear little sparrow," she said in as sweet a voice as she could manage, "how kind you were to my husband."

The sparrow asked her to come in, sat her down and gave her tea and cake. When the old woman got up to go, the sparrow brought out two baskets; one big and heavy, the other small and light. Without even saying "thank you" the old woman grabbed the big basket and hurried through the woods.

As she walked along, the basket grew heavier and heavier. The old woman trudged on, thinking of all the wonderful things that were inside the basket.

At last, she stopped for a rest, put down the basket, and lifted the lid to peek inside. At once, all sorts of horrible things came out. There were slimy snakes,

huge spiders, a wasp that stung her, and horrible crepy crawlies. She screamed and ran home as fast as she could.

When she reached the house, she told her husband what had happened. The old man said nothing. He just looked at her and sighed sadly.

The old woman felt really sorry for what she had done. "I promise I'll never be mean, greedy and bad-tempered ever again," she said, and she kept her promise. From then on, she was always kind and good-tempered, and she always helped the old man feed all the birds that flew into their garden.

A Bag full of Stories

A story from Cambodia

"Please tell me another story. Please," begged Lom. "No, you must go to sleep now," said Lom's old servant. So, Lom snuggled down in bed and thought about the story he had just heard.

Every night, since he had been a very small boy, the old servant had told him wonderful stories - stories about huge giants and powerful wizards, about fierce tigers and wise elephants and about rich emperors and beautiful princesses. Each night it was a new story, and Lom loved to hear them. Lom knew the old servant had been told the stories by his mother, and his grandmother, and his great grandfather, and that the stories were very old.

Lom often boasted to his friends about the stories. "Won't you tell them to us?" they asked again and again. "No," shouted Lom. "They're my stories. I won't tell them to anyone."

123

Now, everyone knows that stories need to be told, and because Lom wouldn't pass them on, they became trapped in an old bag, hanging up in his room.

While Lom was growing up into a handsome man, the old servant still told him a story each night. Then his father arranged for Lom to be married to a pretty girl in the next village. The night before the wedding, the old servant heard a strange whispering in Lom's room. "What can that be?" he muttered. He listened carefully.

The whispering came from the old bag. It was the stories, grumbling to each other. "He's getting married tomorrow," said one. "It's his fault we're all squashed into this old bag."

"He should have let us out," growled another. "We'll make him sorry," squeaked a third. "I've got a plan. Tomorrow, when he's going to the wedding in the next village, he'll get very hot and thirsty. I'll turn myself into a well. When he drinks the water, he'll get a terrible pain in his stomach," said the first story.

"Just in case that doesn't work, I'll turn myself into a watermelon. When he eats it, he'll get a terrible pain in his head," said the second story.

"I'll turn myself into a snake and bite him," said the third. "Then he'll get a terrible pain in his leg." All the stories chuckled and sneered nastily in the bag.

The old servant was horrified. "What am I going to do?" he muttered. "I must stop them somehow. If I warn Lom, he'll think I've gone crazy."

All that night, the servant lay awake, trying to think of a way that he could save Lom.

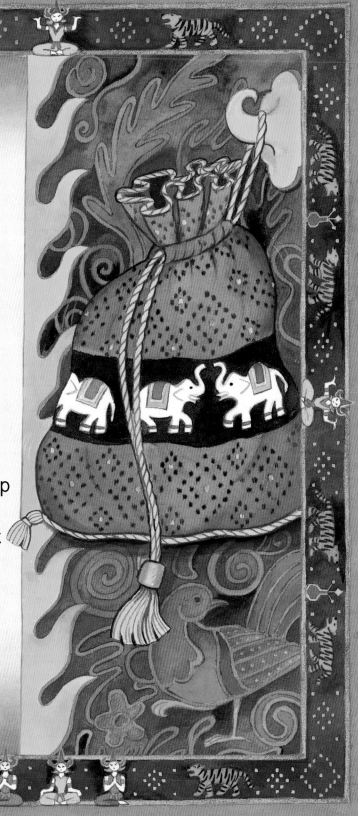

In the morning, just as Lom was setting out on his horse to lead the wedding procession to the next village, the old servant rushed out and grabbed the horse's bridle. With the sun beating down, he led the horse along the road, up the hill, and down the hill to where there was a well.

"Stop," cried Lom, "I'm thirsty, I want a drink," but the old servant led the horse on past the well. Soon they came to a field full of watermelons. "Stop," cried Lom. "I'm hot and thirsty. I want a watermelon." But the old servant would not stop, and on they went.

At the village, crowds of people came out to greet them, waving and cheering. They walked to the bride's house where the wedding ceremony was held. When this was over, there was a great feast for everyone. The old servant was so worried about the snake, he couldn't eat anything. All the time, he was looking everywhere for it but he didn' t see a snake or anything like one.

In the evening, when the wedding guests had gone happily home, Lom and his bride went to their bed chamber. They were alone at last.

Suddenly, there was a loud knocking on the door, and the old servant rushed in, waving a huge stick. "How dare you come bursting in here," shouted Lom. "I'll punish you for this."

The old servant lifted the carpet and there, coiled up on the floor, was a poisonous snake. With one blow, he killed it and flung it out of the room. "How did you know it was there?" cried Lom, holding his frightened new wife in his arms.

The old servant explained about the bag of angry stories, and the harm they had been planning for Lom on his wedding day. "Thank you, thank you, my old friend," said Lom. "I was wrong to keep the stories to myself."

From then on, Lom told the stories to his wife. One by one, they came out of the bag and were happy.

Later, Lom told the stories to his children. His children, of course, told them to their children, and the stories are still being told today.

I know, because I've heard them.

Scandinavia

Germany

Holland

Britain

France

Italy

Spain

Morocco

North America

Mexico

South America

N

W E

S